NEW JEWISH COOKING

NEW JEWISH COOKING

ELIZABETH WOLF COHEN

Quantum Books

A QUANTUM BOOK

Published by Eagle Editions Ltd.
11 Heathfield
Royston
Hertfordshire SG8 5BW

This edition printed 2003

ISBN 1-86160-625-7

QUMTJC

This book is produced by
Quantum Publishing Ltd.
6 Blundell Street
London N7 9BH

Typeset in Great Britain by
Central Southern Typesetters, Eastbourne
Manufactured in Singapore by
Eray Scan (Pte) Ltd.
Printed in Singapore by
Star Standard Industries (Pte) Ltd.

Table of Contents

Introduction
6

Traditional Foods and Condiments
10

Appetizers and Soups
16

Egg Dishes, Blintzes and Pancakes
34

Poultry and Meat Dishes
42

Fish Dishes
63

Accompaniments
71

Salads
88

Baked Goods
103

INTRODUCTION

Jewish cooking, defined by its international scope and kosher requirements, is one of the most interesting and varied cuisines in the world.

Many centuries ago, the Jews were banished from Palestine. They had no state. As the Jews migrated throughout the world, their cooking was borrowed from the local cuisine using native ingredients. While keeping their kosher requirements and observing their holiday customs, each group of Jews developed dishes suited to the country in which they had settled. Middle Eastern Jews, for example, used rice and aromatics with "exotic" vegetables in olive oil and Eastern European Jews salted herrings for use during the long winters and rendered goose or chicken fat for cooking hearty stews and potato kugels.

The main principle differentiating Jewish cooking from any other type of cookery is the principle of kashrut, the Jewish dietary laws commonly known as "kosher cooking". The rules of kashrut were derived from the Bible and Talmud and form a written code. Some of these rules have obvious reasons, others seem arbitrary, but they almost always take local traditions into account. Some say these early theological and symbolic rituals were devised to emphasize the Jews' separateness and oneness with God. In any case, these rules lay down a strict code of practice which is required for choosing and preparing foods, in accordance with holiday customs; this combination creates a distinct Jewish cuisine.

Broadly speaking, Jews fall into two groups, the Ashkenazic and Sephardic, although there are subgroups within each and, in some areas, the boundaries overlap. The Ashkenazic Jews came from Central and Eastern Europe, including Austria, Germany, Hungary, Poland and the former Soviet Union. However, as the Soviet Union was so large, some of the Jews near the Turkish and Iranian borders more closely resemble their Sephardic neighbours in their cooking traditions.

The Sephardic Jews came from Spain, Portugal and the Middle East, During the Spanish Inquisition at the end of the 15th century, many Jews were expelled from Spain and Portugal, some fleeing to Holland, while others returned to the Middle East. Interestingly, cooking slow-simmered stews for the Sabbath was considered by the Spanish as a sign of being Jewish and so a cause for expulsion.

Ashkenazic cooking tends to be subtle and delicate with many well-flavoured, long-cooked dishes of beef and, sometimes, lamb with onions, paprika and sparingly used garlic. Parsley, dill and occasionally chives are the most frequently used herbs. Horseradish is the spicy accompaniment used for meat and fish dishes and always accompanies gefilte fish; pickles and gherkins are a favourite condiment. The combination of vinegar, lemon juice, or sour, and salt with sugar or honey creates a sweet-and-sour combination used in Germany, Hungary, Poland and the states of the former Soviet Union, in dishes such as sweet-and-sour cabbage and stuffed cabbage.

Much of the cooking of Central Europe was based on rendered goose or chicken fat, and smoked or salted fish, as these ingredients were inexpensive and widely available. Once potatoes were introduced from the New World, they became as popular as egg noodles, a speciality of Ashkenazic Jews and the base of many traditional dishes, such as kreplach and kugels. Barley, lentils and kasha are also popular ingredients.

Austrian, Hungarian and German Jews are renowned for their baking. During the great migration, at the end of the 19th century, of Europeans to the United States, German Jews set up bakeries in their adopted homeland. They sold strudels, cakes, yeast-cakes, challah, bagels and other breads and so these are now accepted as Jewish-American foods.

Fruits and vegetables are used widely in Ashkenazic cooking because they are pareve, or neutral, and can be eaten with meat or milk dishes.

In general, Sephardic cooking is characterized by the use of olive oil, lemon and garlic and of highly aromatic and, sometimes, very hot spices. Fresh herbs, such as dill and coriander, are used by Greek and Turkish Jews, but North African Jews prefer cumin and dried ginger. Almost all Sephardic Jews use cinnamon in both savoury and sweet dishes.

Lamb is the favourite meat in most Sephardic kitchens, and saltwater fish is preferred to freshwater. Flat breads, such as pita, are eaten throughout the Middle East and some parts of the Mediterranean, as are olives, aubergines, courgettes, artichokes, tomatoes, peppers and beans. Although desserts are less important in Sephardic cooking than Ashkenazic, eggs and phyllo pastry with walnuts, almonds, cinnamon and rose- or orange-flower waters are more popular than dairy-based sweets.

The cooking of Morocco is particularly refined, influenced by the many years of French occupation. It combines the flavours and foods of the Sephardic tradition with the technical refinements of French cuisine. Spicy and aromatic, with saffron, lemon juice and salt-preserved lemons, garlic,

ABOVE A YEMENITE WITH TYPICAL *PEYOT* (SIDELOCKS) – THE ONLY NON-EUROPEAN JEWS TO WEAR THEM.

coriander, and the "sweet spices" – cinnamon, nutmeg, ginger, mace and allspice – all used generously. Yogurt is used throughout the Middle East, and tahini, a sesame paste, is important in the Eastern Mediterranean and Egypt.

The Jews of Italy, the majority of whom live in one of the oldest areas of Rome, generally cook in the Sephardic tradition, utilizing the many pasta dishes popular in Italian cooking and using the traditional Italian flavourings of rosemary, sage and basil.

In India, the Sephardic traditions are blended with the exotic flavours and spices of cumin, cinnamon, turmeric, cardamom, coriander seeds, garlic, ginger, chillies and fresh coriander. Indian Jews are divided into three groups, the Bene Israel Jews found mainly in Bombay, the Jews of Cochin on the Malibar Coast and the most recent immigrants, the Iraqi Jews. They arrived in the 19th century and settled in Bombay and Calcutta. The Iraqi Jews have combined their use of fresh herbs and greens with the spices and flavourings of India.

The establishment of Israel after World War II has had a tremendous influence on Jewish cooking. The Israelis developed great technological advances in agriculture, food production and the preparation of processed kosher foods. There is an exciting food revolution going on in Israel, led by a new generation of chefs who are working to combine many of the old traditions with the new technology and wide variety of foods now available.

Yemenite Jews from Arabia were among the settlers who flocked into the new Jewish state in 1949. Because they had been isolated for so long from the rest of the Jewish world they retained many of their customs and recipes in a pure form. Their exciting and spicy recipes which use cumin, turmeric, garlic, fresh coriander and a fiery chilli paste, called *Zhoug*, are being incorporated into the Israeli and Jewish repertoire.

With the continual changes and movements of peoples in the Middle East, especially in Israel, Jewish food continues to grow and evolve, while maintaining its traditions and rituals. These factors combine to produce one of the most exciting and satisfying cuisines in the world.

Kashrut — Dietary Laws

Kashrut, the Jewish dietary laws for keeping kosher, or clean and proper, are long and sometimes complicated. Based on Divine Law, they find their roots in the Bible and Talmud, the teachings of Judaism. Keeping kosher is a way of life which involves the selection, preparation and combination of foods in accordance with traditional Jewish ritual and law. It certainly indicates the importance of cooking and food in the life of a Jew!

Meat (Fleishig) and Poultry

In the Torah, the Jewish Bible, kosher animals are defined as quadrupeds which chew the cud and have cloven hooves: beef, veal, lamb, deer and goat are kosher; pork is not. Neither is horsemeat, camel, rabbit or hare. Poultry is kosher; birds of prey, freshly shot pheasant and other game birds, and scavengers are not. Local tradition is also important when determining what is kosher. Some Middle Eastern Jews will not eat geese because "they are of land and sea", yet geese were a staple part of the Eastern European Jews' diet.

For meat and poultry to be kosher, they must be slaughtered in the traditional way by a qualified *shohet*, or slaughterman. A special razor-sharp, smooth knife, twice as long the width of the animal's throat, severs at once the jugular vein, trachea, esophagus and two vagus nerves, causing as little pain and suffering to the animal as possible. The claws and the skin of the feet must also be removed.

As much of the blood as possible is drained away to conform with the Torah's prohibition against the consumption of blood. This is why as much blood as possible must be removed before cooking. This process is generally done by the butcher, but is also done at home to ensure all blood is removed. The meat or poultry is first soaked in cold water for 30 minutes in a receptacle especially for that purpose. It is then rinsed and evenly sprinkled with coarse salt, known as kosher salt, and placed on a perforated draining board for 1 hour. The salt is then shaken off and the meat or poultry rinsed 3 times and drained. Minced meat should be bought koshered or minced after koshering.

Liver and chicken livers require salting, then grilling on a rack or over an open fire to remove all blood and cook the flesh completely. Hearts must be cut open and all veins removed and blood drained before soaking and salting. Nowadays, most kosher meat bought will have been koshered before salting.

Certain parts of the animal are not kosher and cannot be eaten by Jews. Only the forequarters of the permitted quadrupeds are acceptable. The hindquarter meat can be made kosher by "porging", that is removing the veins and sinews, but this process is so time-consuming and expensive it is rarely done.

For recipes in this book, it is assumed that meat and poultry have been koshered in the accepted manner. Therefore these instructions do not appear in each recipe. Where butter or margarine are used, vegetable pareve margarine should be substituted for a kosher recipe. Chicken fat can be replaced with a vegetable-based substitute. All foods and ingredients for recipes should be approved kosher foods; those used in Passover recipes should be approved by the local Union of Orthodox Jewish Congregations or an equivalent body.

Fish and Shellfish

Not all fish are kosher; only fish which have scales and fins are kosher. Shellfish, crustaceans, eels and fish without true scales, such as catfish, monkfish, shark, turbot and sturgeon (therefore, unfortunately, caviar) are not kosher. No special koshering is required for fish; fish is pareve, or neutral.

Meat and Milk

"Thou shalt not seeth a kid in its mother's milk" (Deuteronomy 14:20) provides the basis for the prohibition of eating meat and milk or dairy products together. This was also a way of symbolically rejecting the pagan custom of animal sacrifice; it was also believed to aid digestion. Even now in certain Jewish communities, it is customary to wait up to 6 hours after eating meat before eating foods which contain milk. However, after a milk dish or meal, it is necessary to wait only 1 hour before eating meat.

These laws are observed by keeping separate utensils, cookware, plates, silverware, and even dishwashers! (Glassware can be used for both meat and milk, as it is not porous.) Milk and meat should be stored separately and away from each other in the refrigerator. Milk, or dairy meals, called *milchig*, are meals which contain milk or milk products, such as butter, some margarines, cheese or yogurt. Meat, *fleishig*, refers to meat or poultry dishes. (Milk substitutes such as soya milk can be used for custards, sauces and other foods.)

ABOVE DRIED FRUIT AND NUTS – CHARACTERISTICALLY SEPHARDIC INGREDIENTS.

Pareve Foods

Foods which are neither meat, poultry or milk-based are considered neutral, or pareve. All fruits and vegetables, as well as fish, eggs, vegetable oils and vegetable margarines may be eaten with a meat or milk dish. Eggs must be examined for blood spots; any spot indicates a fertilized egg and the egg must be discarded. It is always advisable to break an egg into a saucer to examine it before adding to any recipe.

Cheese and Gelatine

Natural rennet, which is used to curdle the milk in cheese-making, is produced from the stomach of a ruminating animal – most often a cow. Therefore most natural cheeses are not kosher. Many vegetarian cheeses, however, are made with rennet substitutes and can be eaten. Many new kosher cheeses are coming onto the market. The same is true for gelatine, which is made from animal bones. Kosher gelatine is made from kelp, a seaweed, and is an acceptable substitute. Many non-Jews and vegetarians seek out kosher milk products as they are vegetable-based.

Alcohol

Wine has been drunk by Jews since Biblical times and remains part of the Sabbath ritual, as well as other holidays. Wines and liqueurs containing wine, fermented grapes and/or brandy must be labeled "kosher". To be kosher, the grapes must be harvested and processed under authorized supervision. Nowadays, California, Israel, France and other wine-producing countries produce high-quality kosher wines. Spirits and grain alcohols are also allowed.

Kosher for Passover

During Passover, breads, foods made with yeast, such as beer, flour and other leavening agents are strictly forbidden. These foods are generally replaced with matzo meal or potato flour. Passover customs vary according to local traditions. Sephardic Jews may eat rice, but Ashkenazic Jews may not. In all communities, however, the setting of the Passover Sedar table is special and the choice of foods for this ceremonial dinner has symbolic value. The foods vary from one community and country to another, but wherever Jews are, the rituals are always followed.

Traditional Foods and Condiments

Zhoug
Lebnah
Sephardic Haroset
Ashkenazic Haroset
Beetroot Eingemacts
Schmaltz and Grebenes
Eggs in Salt Water
Tahini Sauce
Horseradish-Beetroot Sauce

ZHOUG

MAKES 125 ML/4 FL OZ

This is a fiery condiment or relish made from chilli paste which is used extensively in Yemenite cooking. It is extremely *hot* and a little goes a long way. Stir this into stews and vegetable dishes for a spicy flavour, or serve as a condiment with pita sandwiches, kebabs or Falafel (see page 23). It can be made with red or green chillies.

- 5 to 6 fresh chilli peppers
- 3 to 4 garlic cloves, peeled
- ¾ teaspoon salt
- Freshly ground black pepper
- 1 teaspoon ground cumin
- ¼ teaspoon ground cardamom

☐ Wearing rubber gloves, core and seed chilli peppers. (Seeds will make it even hotter.)

☐ Into a food processor fitted with metal blade, place chillies and garlic and process until very finely blended. Mixture should be like a paste. Add 1 to 2 tablespoons of water and remaining spices. Process to blend. Store in a tightly covered jar 1 week.

LEBNAH

MAKES ABOUT 750 G/1½ LB

Lebnah is a delicious, soft cream cheese made from yogurt throughout the Middle East. I first tasted it made by an Iranian woman and have been addicted ever since. It has a smooth, creamy texture and slightly acidic taste, which goes well with sweet or savoury foods. Often shaped into balls and preserved in olive oil, lebnah can be bought in Middle Eastern grocery shops, but is easy to make at home.

- 900 ml/1½ pt good-quality plain yogurt
- 1 teaspoon salt
- Olive oil (optional)
- Chopped fresh parsley (optional)

☐ Dampen a double thickness of butter muslin or a clean, thin tea towel and use to line a sieve. Place lined sieve over a large bowl.

☐ Mix yogurt with salt and pour into lined sieve. Cover surface with extended ends of the butter muslin or tea towel and leave in a cool place overnight, or until liquid or whey has stopped dripping.

☐ Unmould on to a shallow dish or bowl and serve as any fresh cheese. Alternatively, with your hands, shape cheese into walnut-size balls. Arrange in a shallow dish and drizzle with olive oil; sprinkle with chopped parsley. Serve with warm pita bread.

SEPHARDIC HAROSET

MAKES ABOUT 625 G/1¼ LB

Haroset is a blend of fruits and nuts served at the Passover sedar to symbolize the mortar and bricks used to build the Egyptian pyramids, and to sweeten the bitter herbs on the Sedar plate. The combinations are innumerable: Ashkenazic recipes usually include apples, almonds or walnuts, cinnamon and wine, while Sephardic versions include dates, walnuts, raisins, oranges, figs, coriander and many other exotic ingredients.

- 90 g/3 oz blanched almonds
- 90 g/3 oz walnut pieces
- 250 g/8 oz fresh dates, stones removed
- 175 g/6 oz raisins
- 1 pomegranate, cut in quarters, seeds removed and juice reserved
- 1 teaspoon ground cinnamon
- ½ teaspoon ground ginger
- ¼ teaspoon cayenne pepper
- ¼ teaspoon ground cloves
- ¼ teaspoon ground cardamom
- 1 to 2 tablespoons orange juice

☐ In a food processor fitted with metal blade, process nuts until coarsely chopped, or finer if you like. Turn into a medium bowl.

☐ Add dates and raisins to processor and, using pulse action, process until chopped, 10 to 15 seconds. Do not overprocess or dried fruit may turn pastey. Add to nuts. Add pomegranate seeds and juice to processor and process until finely chopped.

☐ Stir into nuts and fruit and add the spices. Taste and adjust spices. Moisten with orange juice. Chill before serving.

ABOVE YOU CAN FIND EVERYTHING YOU NEED FOR THE JEWISH TABLE INSIDE THIS TYPICAL NEW YORK CITY DELI.

Ashkenazic Haroset

MAKES ABOUT 550 G/1 LB 2 OZ

- 250 g/8 oz cups walnut pieces or pecan halves
- 2 large dessert apples, quartered and cored but unpeeled
- 2 tablespoons sugar or light brown sugar
- 1 teaspoon ground cinnamon
- ¼ teaspoon ground allspice
- Grated zest and a little juice of 1 lemon
- 2 to 3 tablespoons kosher sweet wine

☐ In a food processor fitted with metal blade, process nuts until coarsely chopped, or finer if you like. Turn into a medium bowl.

☐ Add apple quarters to processor and, using pulse action, process until chopped, 10 to 15 seconds. Do not overprocess or mixture will be too soggy.

☐ Add apple to bowl and stir in remaining ingredients until mixed. Taste and add more sugar or lemon juice if you like. Chill before serving.

BEETROOT EINGEMACTS

MAKES ABOUT 1 KG/2 LB

This preserve is served at Passover, as are many other beetroot dishes in the Ashkenazic repertoire. Although not often seen today, this is easy to make and delicious eaten on matzos with tea as the Ukranian, Lithuanian and Russian Jews used to do. For long-term storage, follow manufacturer's directions on preserving jars; otherwise make a small enough quantity to consume over Passover and store in the refrigerator. A similar preserve can be made with black radishes.

- 250 g/8 oz cup sugar
- 250 ml/8 fl oz honey
- 1 tablespoon ground ginger
- 1.4 kg/3 lb beetroot, cooked, peeled and cut into thin strips or grated
- 2 lemons, cut in half lengthwise, seeds removed and thinly sliced
- 90 g/3 oz cup blanched almonds, chopped

☐ In a large nonmetallic saucepan, over medium-high heat, bring sugar, honey, ginger and 125 ml/4 fl oz water to a boil. Simmer until sugar is completely dissolved and liquid syrupy, 5 to 7 minutes.

☐ Add beetroot strips and lemon slices and stir to blend. Bring to a boil, then reduce heat and cook until mixture is very thick and forms a mass, shaking pan occasionally so mixture does not stick, 30 to 40 minutes. Stir in almonds.

☐ Prepare preserving jars according to manufacturer's directions and spoon mixture carefully into jars. Alternatively, rinse jam jars in water and heat in 180°C/350°F/Gas Mark 4 oven for 5 to 7 minutes. Fill jars with mixture. Cool them and cover with lids. Use within 2 to 3 weeks.

SCHMALTZ AND GREBENES

MAKES ABOUT 60 G/2 OZ

Schmaltz and grebenes have fallen from favour as medical science draws the link between animal fats and coronary heart disease. In Central and Eastern European cooking, schmaltz was rendered from chicken, goose or duck fat and used to cook in as well as to season whole dishes. Old-fashioned chopped chicken liver depended on it. Nowadays, however, we use butter, margarine or oil, but occasionally potatoes fried in schmaltz are for something special. Grebenes are the small pieces of skin or crackling which are also added to chopped liver or potato dishes or eaten on their own like potato crisps.

- Chicken skin
- 250 g/8 oz chicken, goose or duck fat from cavity and outside the bird, cut into small pieces
- ½ onion, chopped (optional)

☐ In a medium saucepan, over low heat, combine chicken skin and fat with 60 ml/2 fl oz cup water. Cook until the fat has melted and water is evaporated. The skin and onion should be crisp and brown. Strain fat (schmaltz) into a small bowl. Drain skin (grebenes) and onion bits on paper towels. Store both covered in refrigerator and use for frying or roasting.

EGGS IN SALT WATER

SERVES 6

This dish was traditionally served only on the Passover Sedar table, to represent the sacrifice to the temple; a symbol of mourning for the death of the Temple, and as a symbol of birth or life. This is an old tradition still used today.

- 3 teaspoons salt
- 6 eggs, hard-boiled and shelled

☐ In a large bowl or soup terrine, combine salt with 900 ml to 1.25 l/1½ to 2 pt water. Stir until dissolved. About 30 minutes before serving add whole eggs; refrigerate until ready to serve. Ladle each egg with a little salt water (125 ml/4 fl oz) in to 6 small bowls and serve to each person.

Tahini Sauce

MAKES ABOUT 250 ML/8 FL OZ

Tahini paste is made from sesame seeds. It is most often used to make a sauce or dip served on the *meze* tables of Greece, Cyprus, Israel and the Middle East. Sold in cans or jars, it is easy to use. A friend of mine, who was born in Cyprus, always serves it as a sauce when we barbecue lamb or chicken. This sauce has a distinct taste and texture which goes well with grilled foods and salads.

- 1 garlic clove, peeled and crushed
- 125 ml/4 fl oz tahini paste
- 60 ml/2 fl oz lemon juice
- ¼ teaspoon salt
- Chopped fresh parsley or coriander for garnish

☐ Rub a small serving bowl with the garlic, then leave garlic in bowl. Add tahini paste and, using a fork, blend in 60 ml/ 2 fl oz water, lemon juice and salt. Wipe edges of bowl and sprinkle with chopped parsley or coriander. Refrigerate until ready to serve.

Horseradish-Beetroot Sauce

MAKES ABOUT 750 ML/1¼ PT

Horseradish, *chrein* in Russian, is considered one of the bitter herbs presented for the Passover table. This sauce is popular with gefilte fish, corned beef and other meats. Fresh horseradish can be found in Chinese supermarkets, and it is like chillies or onions – it can burn your eyes and skin, so wear rubber gloves when preparing it and use a food processor for grating, if possible.

- 1 medium fresh horseradish root
- 3 to 4 beetroot, cooked, peeled, cut to fit food processor tube
- 1 tablespoon light brown sugar or honey
- Freshly ground black pepper
- 175 to 250 ml/6 to 8 fl oz distilled white or cider vinegar

☐ Wearing rubber gloves, use a swivel-vegetable peeler, peel horseradish root. Trim ends. In a food processor fitted with grating disc, grate horseradish.

☐ Without removing processor cover, grate cooked beetroot on to horseradish.

☐ Remove cover and scrape into a medium bowl, mixing well with brown sugar or honey, pepper to taste and vinegar. If mixture is too dry, add a little more vinegar. Store refrigerated in a covered jar.

COOK'S TIP

HORSERADISH VARIES IN PUNGENCY DEPENDING ON THE VARIETY AND ITS AGE, SO TASTE A TINY AMOUNT OF MIXTURE AND ADJUST THE SEASONING ACCORDINGLY.

Appetizers and Soups

Piroshki

Chopped Herring

Herrings in Sour Cream

Chopped Liver

Calves' Foot Jelly

Baba Ganoush

Falafel

Hummus

Artichokes, Jewish Style

Cheese Knishes

Peruvian Pickled Fish

Beetroot Borsht

Sweet-and-Sour Cabbage Soup

Mushroom and Barley Soup

Lentil Soup

Classic Chicken Soup with Matzo Balls

Italian Bean and Pasta Soup

Shchav

PIROSHKI

MAKES ABOUT 38

Piroshki are tiny pastries, originally from Russia, usually eaten with a clear meat or chicken broth, but also delicious on their own. With the tremendous exodus of Russian Jews to America and Israel in recent years, these are becoming increasingly popular; they make a delightful canapé or hors-d'oeuvre. Traditionally made with a yeast-based dough, a good flaky pastry or commercial puff pastry made with vegetable fat can be used. The filling can vary from meat to fish, to mushrooms, to cheese and spinach.

- 1 tablespoon dried yeast
- 1 tablespoon sugar
- 310 ml/10 fl oz lukewarm water
- 375 to 425 g/12 to 14 oz plain flour
- 2 teaspoons salt
- 125 g/4 oz pareve margarine, melted and cooled
- 2 large eggs, lightly beaten
- Vegetable oil for greasing bowl
- 1 egg, beaten with a pinch of salt and sugar, for glaze

MEAT FILLING

- 1 tablespoon vegetable oil
- 1 medium onion, finely chopped
- 250 g/8 oz minced beef or veal
- 1 teaspoon salt
- Freshly ground black pepper
- ¼ teaspoon dried thyme
- ¼ teaspoon grated nutmeg
- 1 egg, lightly beaten

☐ Prepare dough. In a small bowl, combine yeast with sugar and 60 ml/2 fl oz lukewarm water. Leave to stand until mixture begins to foam, 10 to 15 minutes.

☐ In a large bowl, mix 375 g/12 oz of the flour and salt and make a well in centre. Add foamy yeast mixture, remaining water, melted and cooled margarine and beaten eggs. Stir mixture until a soft dough begins to form.

☐ Turn out dough on to lightly floured work surface and knead dough gently, adding a little flour if necessary to keep dough from sticking. Dough will become smooth and slightly elastic after 10 to 15 minutes kneading.

☐ Form dough into ball and place in an oiled bowl. Cover with a clean tea towel and leave in a warm place until dough doubles in bulk, 1 to 1½ hours. Punch down dough, cover and refrigerate overnight. (If dough is needed quickly, cover and leave to rise again in a warm place for about another hour.)

☐ Prepare filling. In a medium frying pan, over medium heat, heat oil. Add chopped onion and cook until onion is soft and begins to colour, about 5 minutes. Add minced beef or veal and cook, stirring occasionally, until meat has lost its pink colour and any liquid has evaporated, 5 to 7 minutes. Season with salt, pepper, thyme, and nutmeg and remove from heat to cool slightly. Mix in the beaten egg, turn into a medium bowl and refrigerate, covered, until ready to use. (Filling can be prepared several hours ahead or overnight.)

☐ Lightly grease 2 large baking sheets (you will need to work in batches). Cut dough into 3 or 4 pieces, work on one piece at a time and keep remaining dough refrigerated.

☐ On a lightly floured surface, roll out dough about 3 mm/⅛ in thick. Using a 7.5 cm/3 in round cutter, cut out as many circles as possible. Brush edge of each circle with a little egg glaze. Place 1 rounded teaspoon of filling on each circle and fold to form a half-moon shape; carefully press edges together. Repeat by rerolling any scraps of dough.

☐ Place on baking sheet, cover with a clean tea towel and leave in a warm place to rise, 20 minutes. Preheat oven to 200°C/400°F/Gas Mark 6.

☐ Brush top of each half-moon with a little egg glaze and bake until golden brown and puffed, 15 to 20 minutes. Serve warm.

COOK'S TIP

PIROSHKI CAN BE MADE AHEAD AND REFRIGERATED. REHEAT IN A 180°C/350°F/GAS MARK 4 OVEN 5 TO 7 MINUTES BEFORE SERVING.

ABOVE DEVOUT JEWS WEARING *TEFILLIN* (BOXES BOUND WITH LEATHER WHICH CONTAIN PASSAGES FROM THE SCRIPTURES) IN A MOSCOW SYNAGOGUE.

Chopped Herring

SERVES 4 TO 6

In the poor Eastern European communities, herring was traditionally eaten after breaking the fast of Yom Kippur to restore salt in the body. Chopped herring is a very popular appetizer among British and South African Jews and is often found on the Friday night table. My South African editor swears by her mother's Chopped Herring. This is her recipe.

- 12 tea biscuits
- 4 Granny Smith apples, quartered and cored but not peeled
- 4 eggs, hard-boiled and quartered
- 4 salted herrings, filleted, skinned and soaked overnight
- 60 ml/2 fl oz distilled white or cider vinegar
- Freshly ground black pepper
- ¼ teaspoon ground cinnamon
- 1 to 2 teaspoons sugar
- Fresh parsley for garnish

COOK'S TIP

MATZOS CAN BE SUBSTITUTED FOR THE TEA BISCUITS IF YOU WISH TO SERVE THE DISH DURING PASSOVER.

☐ In a food processor fitted with metal blade, process tea biscuits until fine crumbs form. Pour into a large bowl. Add apple quarters and, using the pulse action, process until chopped, but not too fine or they will be too mushy. Add to bowl.

☐ Add egg quarters to processor and, using the pulse action, process 3 to 5 times until chopped. Do not overprocess or they will form a paste. Add eggs to bowl. Add herring to processor and process until chopped. Do not overprocess or they will form a paste. Add to bowl and stir.

☐ Stir in the vinegar, pepper to taste, cinnamon and sugar. You may need to taste to adjust the balance of vinegar and sugar. Spread the mixture on a flat serving dish, cover with cling film and refrigerate until ready to serve. Garnish with sprigs of parsley.

Herrings in Sour Cream

SERVES 6 TO 8

Herrings became a staple of the Jewish diet in Poland, Hungary, Czechoslovakia, and other Eastern European countries because they were economical. Herrings of all kinds are available today in Jewish delis. If using salt herrings, soak them in cold water for at least 4 hours.

- 1 500 g/1 lb jar pickled herrings or herrings in wine sauce, drained
- 1 red onion, thinly sliced
- 4 Granny Smith apples, halved and cored but not peeled
- ½ tablespoon lemon juice or cider vinegar
- ½ teaspoon ground cinnamon
- 2 teaspoons sugar
- 250 ml/8 fl oz cream or yogurt
- Freshly ground black pepper
- Radicchio and fresh dill sprigs for garnish
- Black bread for serving

☐ Pat herrings dry with paper towels. Discard onions and liquid from the jar. Lay each herring flat on cutting board and holding sharp knife at an angle, cut each into 5 to 6 diagonal slices. Remove to mixing bowl and add thinly sliced red onion.

☐ Lay each apple half cut-side down on cutting board and cut into thin slices. Add to herrings and onions.

☐ In a small bowl, combine lemon juice or vinegar, cinnamon, sugar and sour cream or yogurt. Season with black pepper.

☐ Pour dressing over herrings, onions and apples. Toss to blend well, cover with cling film and refrigerate 2 hours or overnight.

☐ To serve, arrange a leaf or two of radicchio on individual serving plates, spoon on equal amounts of herring mixture and garnish with sprigs of fresh dill. Serve with black bread.

Chopped Liver

SERVES 6 TO 8

This is probably the best-known and best-loved Jewish dish. No one really knows its origins, but when it comes to chopped liver, everybody's an expert. Traditionally, chicken fat is used to cook the onions and bind the mixture, as well as provide a smooth texture. This version replaces the fat with vegetable oil which is less rich and lower in saturated fat. Use a kosher margarine if you prefer. Serve with rye bread, challah or matzo. For an elegant presentation, pipe on to toast or crackers.

- 500 g/1 lb chicken livers
- Salt
- Freshly ground black pepper
- 2 tablespoons vegetable oil
- 2 medium onions, chopped
- 4 large eggs, hard-boiled and chopped
- Chicken stock (optional)
- Shredded lettuce and cherry tomatoes for garnish

☐ Preheat grill. Arrange livers on foil-lined grill pan and sprinkle with salt. Grill until lightly brown, 3 to 4 minutes. Turn livers over, sprinkle with salt and grill until just cooked through, 3 to 4 minutes longer; livers should no longer be pink. Remove livers to cooling rack to drain and cool slightly.

☐ In a large frying pan, over medium heat, heat oil. Add chopped onions and cook until soft and golden, 10 to 12 minutes, stirring occasionally.

☐ In a food processor fitted with metal blade, chop livers coarsely using the pulse action. Add onions and, using the pulse action, chop until livers and onions are just blended. Add chopped eggs, salt and pepper to taste and, using the pulse action, chop again until just blended. If mixture is dry, add a little more oil or a spoonful of chicken stock.

☐ Spoon mixture into a serving bowl, cover and refrigerate 2 hours or until ready to serve. Garnish with shredded lettuce and cherry tomatoes.

Calves' Foot Jelly

SERVES 8

Love it or hate it, this traditional dish is still very popular with Eastern European Jews. Well made, it resembles some of the more modern, low-fat cooking we prefer today. Mould the mixture in a loaf tin or terrine and serve slices garnished with fresh herbs for a contemporary look. Be sure to have your butcher cut the feet into pieces for easier handling.

- 4 calves' feet, cleaned, halved and cut into pieces
- 500 g/1 lb shin of veal, or 500 g/ 1 lb chicken legs
- 1 large onion, sliced
- 1 carrot
- 1 celery stalk
- 4 bay leaves
- 6 to 8 garlic cloves, peeled and slightly crushed
- 1½ teaspoons salt
- 1 tablespoon black peppercorns
- 2 tablespoons lemon juice or cider vinegar
- 3 to 4 large eggs, hard-boiled and sliced
- Lemon and fresh parsley sprigs for garnish

☐ Place cut-up calves' feet into a very large stockpot and cover with cold water. Over high heat, bring to a boil, then simmer gently for 5 minutes. Drain into a large colander and rinse feet well with cold water.

☐ Place feet in cleaned stockpot and cover again with cold water. Add all remaining ingredients, except lemon juice or vinegar, hard-boiled eggs and garnish. Over high heat, bring to a boil, then simmer for 5 minutes. Using a wet cooking spoon, skim off any froth that comes to the surface.

☐ Partially cover stockpot and simmer gently over low heat for 3 to 4 hours, skimming occasionally. The meat should be very tender and falling off bones.

☐ With a slotted spoon, carefully lift out calves' feet and any meat and remove to a cutting board. Strain liquid into a large heatproof bowl. Wash the pot and return liquid to cleaned pot with lemon juice.

☐ Remove gristle and meat from feet and cut into small pieces. Add meat to liquid.

☐ Ladle half liquid with meat into a terrine or deep dish and refrigerate until the liquid begins to set. Arrange hard-boiled egg slices on surface, pushing them in gently. Carefully spoon over remaining liquid and meat. Refrigerate overnight until firm and set.

☐ To serve, cut jelly from terrine or dish (or turn out on to serving platter.) Garnish with lemon and parsley.

ABOVE THE "BLUE DANUBE" FROM A VANTAGE POINT IN BUDAPEST.

BABA GANOUSH

SERVES 8 TO 10

There are many versions of this aubergine and tahini dip which is popular all over the Middle East. When I lived in a small studio in Paris, I was shocked to learn my Israeli neighbour "grilled" the aubergines directly on the electric hot plate in her even smaller studio.
Ideally, the aubergines should be grilled over a barbecue for 30 to 40 minutes until completely tender, the skins blackened and collapsed; this is what gives the dip its slightly smoky flavour.

- 2 medium aubergines, about 750 g/1½ lb total weight
- 60 ml/2 fl oz lemon juice
- 60 ml/2 fl oz tahini (sesame paste)
- 3 to 4 garlic cloves, peeled and crushed
- Salt
- Freshly ground black pepper
- Olive oil
- Chopped fresh parsley and ripe olives for garnish
- Pita bread, warmed, for serving

☐ Preheat oven to 230°C/450°F/Gas Mark 8. Pierce aubergines all over with a fork or sharp knife. Arrange on a baking sheet and bake until completely tender and collapsed, 30 to 40 minutes. Cool slightly.

☐ Cut each aubergine in half lengthwise and scoop out flesh; place flesh in a food processor fitted with metal blade. Process aubergine until smooth.

☐ Add lemon juice, tahini, garlic and salt and pepper to taste and process until well blended. With the machine running, slowly add 2 to 3 tablespoons olive oil until the mixture is well blended and creamy. Adjust seasoning; spoon into a bowl, cover with cling film, and chill for 2 hours or overnight.

☐ To serve, spoon into a shallow dish or individual plates and with the back of a spoon make a hollow in the centre. Spoon in a little olive oil, sprinkle with chopped parsley and garnish with ripe olives. Serve with warm pita bread.

FALAFEL

MAKES ABOUT 30

These spicy, deep-fried chickpea balls could almost be called the Israeli national dish, although they are also eaten all over the Middle East. They can be eaten on their own, as part of a *meze* or in a pita bread with lettuce, tomato and cucumber. Zhoug and Tahini (see pages 11 and 15) are a must.

- 175 g/6 oz dried chickpeas, soaked at least 12 hours or overnight
- 1 slice day-old white bread, crusts removed
- 1 medium onion, quartered
- 4 to 5 garlic cloves, or to taste
- 2 tablespoons chopped fresh coriander or parsley
- 1 tablespoon ground coriander
- 1 tablespoon ground cumin
- 2 teaspoons salt
- Freshly ground black pepper
- 45 g/1½ oz bulgur, rinsed and drained, or 3 tablespoons plain flour
- 1 teaspoon baking powder
- Vegetable oil for frying
- Pita bread for serving
- Israeli Salad (see page 89), hot pickles, zhoug, and tahini for serving

☐ Drain and rinse the chickpeas. Sprinkle bread with 1 tablespoon water and leave to soak in, then squeeze dry.

☐ In a food processor fitted with metal blade, process chickpeas and bread to a semi-fine paste; you may need to work in batches. Turn mixture into a large bowl.

☐ Into processor, place onion quarters and, using pulse action, process until finely chopped. Add to chickpea purée and scrape processor well. Add garlic cloves to processor and process until finely chopped. Add coriander or parsley to garlic and continue to process until finely chopped. Add mixture to the chickpeas and onions and mix well.

☐ Add ground coriander, cumin, salt and black pepper to taste. Stir in bulgur or flour and baking powder. Using clean hands, mix mixture very well.

☐ Using wet hands, shape about 1 tablespoon of mixture into a ball about the size of a walnut, rounding it between the palms of your hands; set balls on to a baking sheet. Continue shaping until all mixture has been used. (Falafel can be prepared to this point several hours ahead.)

☐ In a deep-fat fryer or deep saucepan, heat oil to 180°C/350°F. Add about one-quarter of the balls, sliding them carefully into the oil. Fry until a rich golden brown, 2 to 3 minutes. Remove with slotted spoon to paper towels to drain. Repeat with remaining balls, one-quarter at a time.

☐ Serve warm in pitas with Israeli Salad or with pickled peppers, zhoug and tahini.

Hummus

SERVES 8 TO 10

This creamy, golden purée of chickpeas is a speciality of Middle Eastern Jews and non-Jews alike. It is popular as an appetizer or one of many dishes in a *meze* of Middle Eastern food. It is worth making a large batch of hummus as it keeps well in the refrigerator and is ideal to serve when unexpected guests arrive.

- 450 g/15 oz dried chickpeas, or 2 cans, well rinsed
- Salt and cayenne pepper
- 4 to 6 garlic cloves, peeled and crushed
- 60 ml/2 fl oz lemon juice
- 60 ml/2 fl oz tahini (sesame paste)
- Olive oil, and chopped fresh parsley for garnish (optional)

☐ Rinse dried chickpeas very well, discarding any broken or discoloured ones. Place in a large bowl and cover generously with cold water; soak 12 hours or overnight.

☐ Transfer chickpeas and their soaking water to a large stockpot and, over medium heat, bring to a boil. Reduce heat and leave to simmer 1½ to 2 hours, until very tender.

☐ Add 1 teaspoon salt and continue simmering for 30 minutes. Drain well, reserving 1 tablespoon of chickpeas and a little cooking liquid.

☐ Press cooked or canned beans through a food mill or sieve, adding reserved cooking liquid, to separate chickpeas from skins. (For a smooth hummus, skins must be separated from chickpeas.) Discard skins.

☐ In a food processor fitted with metal blade, process crushed garlic with a pinch of salt. Add puréed chickpeas and process until smooth. Add the lemon juice, tahini and a pinch of cayenne pepper and purée until finely blended. Hummus should be thick and smooth; add a little more cooking liquid if purée is too thick and adjust the seasoning. Transfer to a bowl and store in the refrigerator, covered, up to 5 days.

☐ To serve, spread hummus in a shallow dish or individual bowls and with the back of a spoon make a hollow in the centre. Chop the reserved chickpeas coarsely and sprinkle over. If wished, pour a little olive oil in the centre of the well, garnish with the chopped chickpeas, parsley and a sprinkling of cayenne pepper.

Artichokes, Jewish Style

SERVES 6

This ancient speciality was introduced to Rome by Jews in the Middle Ages. It should be made with baby artichokes whose chokes have not yet developed, now found in Italian groceries and some large supermarkets. Larger globe artichokes can be used, but the outer leaves and choke should be removed and the stems carefully trimmed.

- Juice of 2 to 3 lemons
- 12 small, young artichokes
- 125 ml/4 fl oz olive oil
- 45 g/1½ oz fresh parsley, chopped (preferably flat leaf)
- 15 g/½ oz basil leaves, torn
- 1 teaspoon salt
- Freshly ground black pepper
- 8 to 10 garlic cloves, peeled and finely chopped
- Matzo meal
- Olive oil for frying
- Fresh parsley sprigs or basil leaves for garnish

☐ Place lemon juice in a large bowl and add enough water to fill bowl halfway.

☐ Discard any tough or damaged outer leaves from the artichokes. With a sharp knife, trim tops off artichokes and peel stalks if necessary; cut stalks to 5 to 7.5 cm/2 to 3 in. As you prepare each artichoke, place it in bowl of water to prevent discoloration. Add more water if necessary.

☐ In a small bowl, combine olive oil, parsley, basil, salt, pepper to taste and garlic. Place 90 g/3 oz of matzo meal in a pie plate; set aside.

☐ Drain artichokes well and pat dry with paper towels. Holding each artichoke by its stalk, bang each top against a work surface to spread open leaves. Holding each by its stalk, spoon a little oil and herb mixture between leaves, then roll each artichoke in the matzo meal.

☐ Cover bottom of a large casserole or heavy frying pan with about 3 mm/⅛ in olive oil; heat over medium heat. Place artichokes in pan and cook, covered, over medium-low heat, until tender and golden, 25 to 30 minutes, turning once or twice. Serve at room temperature with any cooking juices spooned over or drizzle with additional olive oil. Garnish with fresh parsley sprigs or basil leaves.

ABOVE HUMMUS.

Cheese Knishes

MAKES ABOUT 2 DOZEN

Knishes, tiny filled pastries, are multipurpose, traditional Ashkenazic fare. Sometimes served with soup or on their own as an appetizer they are traditionally eaten at Shavuot with a moist cheese filling. Other fillings include potato and kasha (buckwheat). Many different kinds of pastry can be used but this sour cream pastry made in the food processor makes the whole job quick and easy.

PASTRY

- 250 g/8 oz plain flour
- 1 teaspoon baking powder
- ½ teaspoon salt
- 1 teaspoon icing sugar
- 125 g/4 oz unsalted butter or hard margarine, cut into small pieces
- 75 ml/2½ fl oz sour cream
- 1 egg, beaten, to glaze

CHEESE FILLING

- 250 g/8 oz tub cottage cheese
- 2 tablespoons sour cream
- 2 tablespoons fine matzo meal
- 1 tablespoon sugar
- 1 tablespoon melted butter
- 2 eggs, beaten
- 45 g/1½ oz sultanas, or 1 tablespoon chopped fresh parsley

☐ Into a large bowl, sift flour, baking powder, salt and sugar. Transfer to a food processor fitted with metal blade. Add butter and process until mixture resembles fine crumbs. Remove cover and spoon the sour cream evenly over flour-butter mixture. Using pulse action, process until mixture begins to hold together. Do not allow dough to form into a ball or pastry will be tough. If dough appears too dry, add a little cold water, 1 tablespoon at a time.

☐ Turn out dough on to lightly floured work surface and knead lightly. Form dough into a ball and flatten; wrap well and refrigerate 2 hours or overnight. Leave dough to soften 15 minutes at room temperature before rolling out.

☐ In a large bowl, combine all filling ingredients until well blended.

☐ Grease 2 large baking sheets. Cut dough in half and work with one half at a time. Roll out dough to a 20 × 30 cm/8 × 12 in rectangle about 3 mm/⅛ in thick. Cut dough into 10 cm/4 in squares. Place filling in centre of each square.

☐ Brush edges of each square with a little egg glaze and fold lower-left corner up to upper-right corner to form a triangle. Using a fork, press edges together to seal well. Place on baking sheet. Continue with remaining dough and filling. You will need to bake in batches.

☐ Preheat oven to 200°C/400°F/Gas Mark 6. Brush each triangle with a little egg glaze and score top of pastry to let steam escape. Bake until a rich golden brown, 17 to 20 minutes. Cool 15 minutes before serving.

COOK'S TIP

Smaller knishes can be made by using a 7.5 cm/3 in round cutter and cutting circles from pastry. Fold over 1 spoonful of filling to make a half-moon shape and proceed as above.

POTATO FILLING

Fry 1 finely chopped onion in 15 g/½ oz chicken fat, butter or margarine. Stir in 500 g/1 lb mashed potatoes. Remove from heat, cool slightly. Beat in 1 egg and salt and pepper to taste, cool before using.

PERUVIAN PICKLED FISH

SERVES 4 TO 6

This very contemporary fish dish, also known as ceviche, is popular with Jews in Central and South America. Any firm white fish can be used, as well as salmon and sea trout. The acid in the lime and lemon juice has a similar effect to heat; the fish is effectively cooked.

- 1 kg/2 lb sole, halibut or red snapper fillets, or any combination of firm-fleshed, non-oily fish
- 250 ml/8 fl oz fresh lemon juice
- 250 ml/8 fl oz fresh lime juice
- 2 red chillies, thinly sliced
- 2 red onions, thinly sliced
- 1 to 2 garlic cloves, peeled and finely chopped
- Kosher salt to taste
- Freshly ground black pepper to taste
- Fresh coriander leaves for garnish

☐ Cut fish fillets into 2.5 cm/1 in strips; place in a large, shallow nonmetallic dish.

☐ In a large bowl, combine the remaining ingredients, except garnish. Pour marinade over the fish strips, spreading evenly over fish. Refrigerate at least 3 hours, or until the fish strips turn white and opaque. (Do not marinate much longer or the fish will begin to fall apart as the acids continue to break down the proteins.)

☐ Serve a few fish strips with some chilli and onion slices on individual plates and garnish with coriander leaves.

Beetroot Borsht

SERVES 6

There are many versions of borsht; the only ingredient which does not vary is the beetroot! This soup is made all over Eastern Europe and served hot or cold. It can be made with beef or without, with vegetables or without, and served chunky or smooth.

This elegant ruby-red purée is most delicious served with a swirl of sour cream, snipped chives and dill, and for an extra treat, serve with small boiled potatoes.

- 750 g/1½ lb small beetroot with tops
- 1 onion, chopped
- 900 ml/1½ pt vegetable stock or water
- 1 teaspoon salt
- Freshly ground black pepper
- 3 tablespoons fresh lemon juice or cider vinegar
- 2 tablespoons light brown sugar, or to taste
- Sour cream for serving
- Snipped fresh chives and dill for garnish

☐ Cut tops from beetroot, leaving 5 to 7.5 cm/2 to 3 in of stalk attached. Scrub beetroot thoroughly under cold running water, being sure to remove all grit and sand. If tops are young and tender they may be added, well washed.

☐ In a large saucepan, over medium heat, place beetroot and chopped onion and cover with stock or water. Bring to a boil, then simmer, partially covered, until beetroot is tender, 20 to 30 minutes. Carefully strain liquid through a sieve into a large heatproof bowl; rinse saucepan.

☐ Remove beetroot and peel off skin. Quarter beetroot and add to a food processor fitted with metal blade. Add onions (and tops if using) from sieve to the beetroot; process until finely puréed.

☐ Return beetroot and onion purée to washed saucepan and add reserved cooking liquid, being careful not to add any sand or grit which may have settled on bottom.

☐ Over medium heat, bring soup to a boil. Season with salt, pepper, lemon juice or vinegar and brown sugar. Simmer 5 minutes and serve hot with a swirl of sour cream. Sprinkle with fresh chives and dill. Alternatively, cool and chill to serve cold.

COOK'S TIP

IF SERVING COLD, RESEASON BEFORE SERVING AND THIN WITH A LITTLE WATER IF NECESSARY.

Sweet-and-Sour Cabbage Soup

SERVES 8

The combination of sweet and sour is very popular in Eastern-European Jewish cuisine. Perhaps this is why Jews are so fond of those flavours in Chinese food!

- 1 kg/2 lb brisket of beef
- 1 marrow bone (optional if unobtainable)
- 2 onions, chopped
- 2 carrots, finely chopped
- 2 large tomatoes, peeled, seeded, and chopped
- 1 small cabbage, quartered, cored and finely shredded
- 90 g/3 oz raisins
- Juice of 2 lemons
- 60 g/12 oz light brown sugar
- Salt
- Freshly ground black pepper

☐ In a large casserole or saucepan, place beef, bone if using, and 2 l/3¼ pt water. Over medium-high heat, bring to a boil. Skim off any foam which comes to the surface and boil for 5 minutes, skimming as necessary. Reduce heat and simmer 1 hour.

☐ Add chopped onions, carrots and tomatoes and continue cooking until meat is tender, at least 1 hour longer. Remove meat and marrow bone.

☐ Add shredded cabbage and raisins to soup. Cover and simmer until cabbage is just tender, 20 to 30 minutes; add a little water if soup has reduced too much.

☐ Meanwhile, cut or shred meat into small pieces. Discard marrow bone. Add meat pieces to soup with lemon juice, sugar, salt and pepper to taste. Adjust sweet-and-sour balance to your taste. Simmer 10 minutes longer and serve hot.

ABOVE Beetroot Borsht.

Mushroom and Barley Soup

SERVES 8

Wild mushrooms were easily found in the damp woodlands of Eastern Europe, and this soup is a favourite with Jews from that area. Often made with a beef base, this is a vegetarian version, but either way it is a rich and satisfying soup thickened by the barley and flavoured with mushrooms. A little dill sprinkled over the top makes a delicious garnish.

- 60 g/2 oz dried mushrooms (see Note)
- 1 tablespoon vegetable oil
- 1 onion, finely chopped
- 2 carrots, finely chopped
- 1 small turnip, peeled and finely chopped
- 500 g/1 lb button mushrooms, chopped
- 250 g/8 oz pearl barley
- 1 teaspoon salt
- Freshly ground black pepper
- Chopped fresh dill for garnish

☐ In a small bowl, place dried mushrooms. Cover with hot water and soak for 20 minutes. (Alternatively, follow directions on package.)

☐ Meanwhile, in a large casserole or saucepan, heat oil. Add onion and cook until softened, 3 to 5 minutes. Add carrots, turnip, button mushrooms and barley. Cover vegetables with cold water.

☐ Over high heat, bring to a boil. Skim off any foam which comes to the surface, reduce heat and simmer until vegetables and barley are just tender, 30 to 35 minutes; you may need to add more water.

☐ Using a slotted spoon, carefully remove dried, soaked mushrooms from their soaking liquid; do not pour liquid over them as any sand will not be left behind. Slice mushrooms and add to soup.

☐ Strain soaking liquid through a butter muslin-lined sieve and add to soup. Continue cooking more until flavours are blended, 20 to 30 minutes. Serve hot, garnished with chopped fresh dill.

NOTE

USE CÈPE OR PORCINI DRIED MUSHROOMS; DO NOT USE CHINESE OR JAPANESE DRIED MUSHROOMS. CÈPES OR PORCINI ARE OFTEN AVAILABLE DRIED FROM GOURMET SUPERMARKETS AND SPECIALITY SHOPS. THEY HAVE A STRONGER FLAVOUR THAN FRESH MUSHROOMS.

Lentil Soup

SERVES 8

Jewish folklore claims that this is the soup for which Esau sold his birthright. That may be an exaggeration, but this soup is very popular in Israel and as a warming winter soup throughout Eastern Europe. Use red lentils if you can find them, because the colour is rich and tempting and they do not need presoaking. For a pareve soup, use vegetable oil and water or a vegetable stock.

- 2 tablespoons chicken fat
- 2 onions, finely chopped
- 2 stalks celery, finely chopped
- 2 carrots, finely chopped
- 375 g/12 oz red or brown lentils (if using brown lentils, follow directions on package for soaking)
- 2 l/3¼ pt beef stock or water
- Salt
- Freshly ground black pepper
- 1 teaspoon grated nutmeg or ground cloves
- Chopped fresh parsley for garnish

☐ In a large casserole or saucepan, over medium heat, melt chicken fat. Add onions and cook until softened and just beginning to colour, 3 to 5 minutes. Add celery, carrots and lentils. Add beef stock and enough water to cover generously.

☐ Bring to a boil and skim off any foam which comes to the surface. Reduce heat, cover and simmer until vegetables and lentils are tender, 45 to 50 minutes, adding a little more water if necessary. (Brown lentils may take longer to cook.)

☐ Into a food processor fitted with metal blade, ladle half the soup. Process until puréed. Return purée to soup. Season with salt and pepper to taste and add grated nutmeg or ground cloves. Serve hot, garnished with chopped parsley.

CLASSIC CHICKEN SOUP WITH MATZO BALLS

SERVES 8 TO 10

Chicken soup, also known as "Jewish pencillin", is thought by Jewish mothers to cure all ills! It is a simple soup made all over the world and the seasonings used reflect its regional origins. Matzo balls are one of the most popular accompaniments but noodles, rice, tiny matzo squares, flour-based dumplings (kreplach), can all be added.

- 1 large boiling fowl, about 2.25 kg/5 lb quartered (ask butcher to include giblets, neck and feet, but not livers)
- 3 carrots, cut into pieces
- 2 medium onions, a few skins reserved
- 2 stalks celery
- 3 leeks, split and well rinsed
- 1 ripe tomato, quartered and seeded
- 2 garlic cloves, peeled
- 2 chicken stock cubes (optional)
- 1 tablespoon black peppercorns
- 1 teaspoon salt
- Stems from 1 small bunch fresh parsley
- Chopped fresh parsley for garnish

MATZO BALLS (KNEIDLACH)

- 125 g/4 oz medium matzo meal
- ½ teaspoon salt
- ½ teaspoon freshly ground black pepper
- ¼ teaspoon ground ginger
- ¼ teaspoon ground cinnamon
- 250 ml/8 fl oz boiling water
- 2 tablespoons blanched almonds, very finely ground
- 2 tablespoons chicken fat or chicken-flavoured vegetable fat
- 1 egg, lightly beaten

☐ Remove any excess fat from inside and outside of chicken. (Chicken fat can be discarded or rendered for schmaltz, see page 14.) Remove any yellow or green bits from giblets. Place chicken pieces, giblets, neck and feet in a large bowl. Pour over boiling water; drain. Scrape off any hard skin from feet.

☐ Place chicken pieces, neck and feet in a large stockpot and cover with cold water. Over high heat, bring to a boil, then skim off any foam which comes to the surface. Add giblets and remaining soup ingredients, except parsley for garnish, and bring to a boil, skimming off any more foam which comes to surface. Reduce heat to low and simmer about 3 hours.

☐ Strain soup into a large heatproof bowl, reserving chicken pieces and giblets. Cool soup, then refrigerate, covered, overnight. Remove meat from the chicken bones and cut into small pieces. Cut giblets into small pieces and add to chicken pieces. Refrigerate, covered, overnight.

☐ Prepare matzo balls. In a large bowl, mix matzo meal with salt, pepper, ginger and cinnamon. Pour boiling water over and stir. Add finely ground almonds, chicken fat or chicken-flavoured vegetable fat and beaten egg. Mix and refrigerate at least 2 hours.

☐ To serve, remove cold soup from refrigerator and carefully remove any congealed fat from the surface. Transfer to a large saucepan, add cut-up chicken and giblets and bring to a boil.

☐ Remove matzo-ball mixture from refrigerator. Scoop out mixture and form into 2.5 cm/1 in balls, rolling mixture between wet palms of hands. Drop balls into simmering soup and cook until matzo balls are floating and puffed, 20 to 30 minutes. Do not let soup boil or balls will fall apart.

☐ Stir in chopped fresh parsley and serve immediately.

ABOVE FRESH FRUIT AND VEGETABLES FOR SALE IN MINORCA, SPAIN.

Italian Bean and Pasta Soup

SERVES 6

Bean soups are popular with most Jewish communities. Ashkenazic and Sephardic seasonings vary but chunky, flavourful soups are always welcome as a first course or light meal. This Jewish–Italian soup is scented with sage, rosemary and basil.

- 215 g/7 oz dried haricot or cannellini beans, soaked at least 8 hours
- 2 tablespoons olive oil
- 1 onion, finely chopped
- 1 stalk celery, finely chopped
- 1 carrot, finely chopped
- 500 g/1 lb fresh tomatoes, peeled, seeded and chopped, or 2 425 g/14 oz cans plum tomatoes, drained and chopped
- 3 to 4 garlic cloves, peeled and crushed
- 2 chicken or vegetable stock cubes, crumbled
- 2 bay leaves
- 2 teaspoons dried rosemary, crumbled
- 1 teaspoon dried sage, crumbled
- 125 g/4 oz small pasta shapes, such as shells, bows or wheels
- 3 tablespoons chopped fresh parsley
- 3 tablespoons shredded fresh basil leaves
- Salt
- Freshly ground black pepper
- Fresh basil leaves for garnish

☐ Drain soaked beans. In a large casserole or saucepan, combine beans and 900 ml/1½ pt water. Over high heat, bring to a boil. Skim off any foam which comes to the surface, reduce heat and simmer until beans are tender, 1 to 1½ hours. Add water so beans remain covered. Remove from heat.

☐ In another large saucepan, over medium heat, heat olive oil. Add chopped onion and cook until onion begins to soften, 4 to 5 minutes. Add chopped celery and chopped carrot and continue cooking 4 to 5 minutes longer. Add chopped tomatoes, garlic, stock cubes, bay leaves, rosemary and sage and bring to a boil.

☐ Cook, uncovered, until vegetables are tender, about 5 minutes. Add cooked beans and 900 ml/1½ pt cooking liquid (make up liquid with water, if necessary).

☐ Bring soup to a boil. Add pasta and cook, uncovered, until pasta is tender, 8 to 10 minutes. Stir in chopped parsley and shredded basil. Season with salt and freshly ground black pepper. Garnish each portion with a fresh basil leaf.

Shchav

SERVES 8

This is a Russian soup made from sorrel, also called "sour grass", which is generally served cold. Sorrel can be difficult to find unless you are lucky enough to grow it in your garden, but young spinach leaves make a good substitute, although they lack the sharpness of the sorrel leaves. This soup was frequently served on Shavuot.

- 500 g/1 lb sorrel or young spinach leaves, well rinsed and coarsely chopped
- 1 bunch watercress, chopped
- 1 onion, chopped
- 1 stalk celery, finely chopped
- 2 l/3¼ pt vegetable stock (optional)
- Juice and grated zest of 1 lemon
- 2 or 3 tablespoons sugar
- Salt
- Freshly ground black pepper
- Sour cream and fresh dill sprigs for garnish

☐ Into a large casserole or saucepan, place sorrel or spinach, watercress, onion and celery. Pour in 2 l/3¼ pt vegetable stock or water. Over high heat, bring to a boil, then simmer partially covered, 20 minutes, until watercress is just tender. Cool slightly.

☐ Into a blender or food processor, ladle soup. Blend or process until finely puréed. Return soup to pan and add lemon juice and zest, sugar, salt and pepper to taste. Pour into a nonmetallic container and cool completely. Refrigerate at least 3 to 4 hours or until ready to serve.

☐ Serve Shchav chilled in chilled bowls, topped with a dollop of sour cream and sprig of dill.

ABOVE ITALIAN BEAN AND PASTA SOUP.

Egg Dishes, Blintzes and Pancakes

Haminados

Egg and Onion

Scrambled Eggs with Lox

Matzo Brei

Orange-Challah French Toast

Blinis with Smoked Salmon and Sour Cream

Cheese Blintzes with Strawberries

Persian Pancakes with Yogurt

HAMINADOS

SERVES 8

These slow-cooked eggs are a typical Sephardic Passover dish. They are sometimes cooked in a stew, such as hamin or dfina, but are simple to do on their own. Serve as an appetizer, sliced in salads or at barbecues or picnics with hummus. The onion skins give the eggs their golden-brown colour.

- 8 large eggs
- Skins of 8 onions
- 1 teaspoon salt
- ½ teaspoon freshly ground black pepper
- 2 tablespoons olive oil
- Hummus for serving (see page 24)

☐ Preheat oven to 180°C/350°F/Gas Mark 4. Into a small ovenproof casserole, place all ingredients, except hummus; add enough water to cover. Cover tightly and place in the oven. Immediately reduce heat to minimum, about 100°C/200°F/Gas Mark ¼, and bake for 6 to 8 hours or overnight.

☐ Rinse and drain eggs. They can be served warm or chilled with a little hummus on the side.

Egg and Onion

SERVES 6

This simple egg dish is a favourite appetizer, especially with English Jews. It is often served as a simple, easy-to-do appetizer for a Sabbath dinner, or used as a sandwich filling. It can be made with raw or cooked onions, or spring onions which have a milder flavour. It is delicious with rye or black bread. This is my neighbour's recipe. She serves it with matzos.

- 1 large onion, quartered
- 8 eggs, hard-boiled and quartered
- 2 to 3 tablespoons soft margarine or chicken-flavoured vegetable fat
- Salt
- Freshly ground black pepper
- Fresh parsley sprigs for garnish

☐ In a food processor fitted with metal blade, place onion. Process until finely chopped. Replace metal blade with plastic blade, and add egg quarters and chicken-flavoured vegetable fat or margarine. Using pulse action, process until coarsely chopped but well blended. Do not overprocess. Season with salt and pepper and process 2 to 3 seconds.

☐ Turn into a serving dish and refrigerate until ready to serve. Garnish with parsley before serving.

COOK'S TIP

SERVE IN SCOOPS WITH STRIPS OF SMOKED SALMON OR LOX TO GARNISH.

ABOVE YOUNG GIRL HELPS IN THE FIELDS OF ONE OF ISRAEL'S MANY KIBBUTZIM.

Scrambled Eggs with Lox

SERVES 4

This is a favourite brunch dish which is easily prepared ahead and then cooked at the last minute. Small pieces of lox or smoked salmon are often available at Jewish delis at a reasonable price, and a little goes a long way in this dish. Other smoked fish, such as herring or haddock, can be substituted.

- 60 g/2 oz butter or margarine
- 1 large onion, cut in half and thinly sliced
- 10 large eggs
- Salt
- Freshly ground black pepper
- 250 g/8 oz lox or smoked salmon, diced
- Fresh parsley sprigs for garnish

☐ In a large frying pan, over a medium-low heat, melt 30 g/1 oz butter or margarine. Add onion and cook until softened and lightly golden, 8 to 10 minutes.

☐ In a large bowl, whisk eggs with salt and pepper to taste. Melt remaining butter or margarine in frying pan with onions and add egg mixture. Reduce heat to low and scramble eggs gently, stirring constantly.

☐ Just before eggs are set, gently stir in diced lox or smoked salmon. Serve immediately, garnished with parsley.

MATZO BREI

Matzo brei is a dairy dish which is kosher for Passover. It is quick and easy, and the children love it. Serve with apple sauce and sour cream.

- 2 whole matzos
- 125 ml/4 fl oz milk or water
- 2 eggs, well beaten
- Salt
- Freshly ground black pepper
- ¼ teaspoon ground cinnamon (optional)
- 30 g/1 oz butter or pareve margarine
- Sugar and ground cinnamon for sprinkling
- Apple sauce and sour cream for serving

☐ Into a large shallow bowl, break matzos into small pieces. Pour over milk or water and leave to stand until matzos are softened and milk is partly absorbed, about 5 minutes.

☐ Beat in eggs, salt and pepper to taste and cinnamon if using.

☐ In a medium frying pan, over medium heat, melt butter or margarine. Add egg and matzo mixture and cover. Cook until underside is golden brown, 10 minutes. With a palette knife, carefully turn over and cook 3 minutes longer or until brown. Serve in wedges with a sprinkling of sugar and cinnamon. Accompany it with apple sauce and sour cream.

Orange-Challah French Toast

SERVES 6

My favourite recipe for French toast. The challah should be cut quite thick and left to soak in the egg mixture so that when it is cooked the outside is brown and crisp but the inside remains soft and moist. Serve with maple syrup or dust with icing sugar.

- 4 eggs, well beaten
- ½ teaspoon salt
- 2 tablespoons sugar
- 250 ml/8 fl oz orange juice
- ½ teaspoon vanilla extract
- 125 to 250 ml/4 to 8 fl oz milk
- 12 slices challah bread, each about 2 cm/¾ in thick
- Butter for frying, melted
- Maple syrup or icing sugar for serving
- Orange slices for garnish (optional)

☐ In a large shallow baking dish, beat eggs with salt, sugar, orange juice, vanilla and 125 ml/4 fl oz milk. (Depending on the size of the bread, you may need to add a little more milk.)

☐ Lay slices of bread in egg mixture and leave to stand 2 minutes. Turn bread slices over and leave to soak until egg mixture is completely absorbed, about 5 minutes longer.

☐ In a large frying pan or on a griddle, over medium heat, melt 45 g/1½ oz butter. Add slices of soaked bread and cook until underside is golden brown, 3 to 5 minutes. Using a palette knife, turn bread slices and cook until brown, 1 to 2 minutes longer.

☐ Serve immediately with maple syrup or icing sugar. Garnish with orange slices.

Blinis with Smoked Salmon and Sour Cream

SERVES 6

Blinis are Russian pancakes made with buckwheat flour. They have a nutty flavour which is enhanced by smoked salmon or lox and sour cream. A less extravagant presentation can be offered with chopped radishes and cucumber, spring onions and capers. Blinis make a wonderful brunch, light lunch or supper dish.

- 60 ml/2 fl oz lukewarm water
- 1½ teaspoons dried yeast
- 60 g/2 oz plain flour
- 90 g/3 oz buckwheat flour
- ½ teaspoon salt
- 250 ml/8 fl oz milk
- 2 eggs, separated
- 60 g/2 oz butter or margarine
- 4 spring onions, thinly sliced on the diagonal
- 125 ml/4 fl oz sour cream
- Snipped fresh chives for garnish
- 2 tablespoons sour cream
- 125 g/4 oz smoked salmon or lox, thinly sliced

COOK'S TIP

BLINIS CAN BE MADE USING PLAIN FLOUR, BUT THE FLAVOUR AND TEXTURE IS MUCH BETTER USING BUCKWHEAT FLOUR. IT IS AVAILABLE IN HEALTH-FOOD SHOPS AND LARGE SUPERMARKETS.

☐ Into a small bowl, pour lukewarm water and sprinkle yeast over water. Leave to stand until yeast becomes foamy and bubbly, 5 minutes.

☐ Into a large bowl, sift plain flour, buckwheat flour and salt; make a well in centre. Heat 175 ml/6 fl oz of the milk to lukewarm and add it to well with yeast mixture, stirring with a wire whisk and drawing in flour little by little to form a smooth batter. Cover bowl with a clean tea towel and leave in a warm place until batter becomes light and bubbly, 3 hours.

☐ Beat remaining 60 ml/2 fl oz milk into batter; beat egg yolks and stir into batter with half butter, melted, and sour cream.

☐ In another bowl, with a hand-held mixer at medium speed, beat egg whites until stiff peaks form (do not overbeat). Fold egg whites into blini batter until just blended. (Do not overblend; a few white lumps will cook out.)

☐ In a large frying pan or on a griddle, over medium-high heat, melt remaining butter. Using a small ladle, pour batter into pan or griddle to form small pancakes. Cook until undersides are lightly browned, about 2 minutes. Turn blinis over and cook 1 to 2 minutes longer. Continue until all batter is used, adding more butter if necessary. (Keep blinis warm in a 150°C/300°F/Gas Mark 2 oven if necessary.)

☐ Arrange blinis on individual plates or on a large serving dish. Divide smoked salmon or lox slices equally on to blinis. Top each blini with a few sliced spring onions and a spoonful of sour cream. Sprinkle with chives and serve warm.

ABOVE Blinis with Smoked Salmon and Sour Cream.

CHEESE BLINTZES WITH STRAWBERRIES

SERVES 6 TO 8

Blintzes are a symbol of Jewish cooking around the world, with the name coming from the Yiddish for pancake. It is a simple crêpe or pancake filled with cheese or fruits or savoury fillings such as potato and mushroom, chicken livers, cabbage or meat. The blintze, filled with cheese and topped with fruit, is a staple meal in Jewish dairy restaurants and makes an ideal choice for a milk meal at Passover, Shavuot or any time.

- 3 large eggs
- ½ teaspoon salt
- ½ teaspoon sugar
- 30 g/1 oz butter or margarine, melted
- 375 ml/12 fl oz milk or water
- 75 g/2½ oz plain flour
- Butter or margarine for baking or frying, melted

FILLING

- 500 g/1 lb rich cottage cheese or cottage cheese
- 175 g/6 oz cream cheese, softened
- 60 g/2 oz sugar
- 1 teaspoon vanilla extract
- 500 g/1 lb strawberries, thawed if frozen
- Sugar
- Juice and grated zest of 1 lemon

☐ In a large bowl, beat eggs, salt, sugar, melted butter or margarine and milk or water until well blended.

☐ Into a medium bowl, sift flour; make a well in centre. Using a wire whisk, gradually stir beaten egg mixture into flour, drawing in flour from edges of well until all egg mixture is added. Whisk until smooth. Strain into a measuring jug. Cover and refrigerate about 1 hour. (Batter may thicken; add milk or water to thin if necessary.)

☐ Over medium heat, heat a 17.5 cm/7in crêpe pan or frying pan. Brush with a little melted butter. Pour 3 to 4 tablespoons (about 60 ml/2 fl oz) batter into crêpe pan, tipping pan to coat bottom with batter. Cook until top looks set and bottom is lightly browned, about 2 minutes. Using a palette knife, loosen edges and flip crêpe, then cook 10 seconds. Slip cooked blintze on to a piece of greaseproof paper. Repeat until all batter is used, stacking blintzes between sheets of greaseproof paper. (Blintzes can be used immediately or stored in the refrigerator or frozen.)

☐ Preheat oven to 180°C/350°F/Gas Mark 4. Brush a 37.5 × 25cm/15 × 10 in Swiss roll tin with butter or margarine.

☐ Make filling. In a medium bowl, with a mixer at medium speed, beat cottage cheese, cream cheese, sugar and vanilla until smooth.

☐ On a clean work surface, spread 1 heaped tablespoon of cheese mixture down centre of each blintze. Fold sides towards centre, so each side covers about half the filling. Beginning at bottom edge, roll up blintze. Arrange seam-side down on buttered tin. Brush each folded blintze with a little butter and bake until heated through, about 10 minutes.

☐ Reserve 6 to 8 strawberries, slice each in half lengthwise and set aside. Hull remainder. Into a food processor, fitted with metal blade, place half of the strawberries. Add sugar to taste and lemon juice and grated zest. Process until smooth and pour into small bowl. Chop remaining strawberries and add to purée. Add more sugar if necessary.

☐ To serve, place 2 blintzes on a plate, spoon over a little strawberry sauce and garnish with 2 strawberry halves.

NOTE

FOR PASSOVER, THE BLINTZE BATTER CAN BE MADE WITH POTATO FLOUR AND WATER. THE MIXTURE WILL BE SLIGHTLY THINNER AND WILL MAKE A CRISPER BLINTZE.

PERSIAN PANCAKES WITH YOGURT

SERVES 4

My friend Sheema comes from the border area of Pakistan and Iran. She makes these delicious "green" pancakes which are like a fritter. They can be eaten on their own with yogurt or cream cheese, or as an accompaniment to spicy curries, which is how she often serves them.

- 400 g/13 oz spinach, Swiss chard or watercress, chopped
- 2 large sprigs each fresh coriander, parsley and dill
- 2 small leeks, or 4 large spring onions, thinly sliced
- 6 eggs, beaten
- Salt
- Freshly ground black pepper
- ¼ teaspoon grated nutmeg
- 125 g/4 oz matzo meal
- Vegetable oil for frying
- Yogurt, sour cream or cream cheese for serving
- Fresh coriander or dill for garnish

☐ In a food procesor fitted with metal blade, process spinach, Swiss chard or watercress, herbs and leeks or spring onions until smooth. Turn into a large bowl. Add beaten eggs, salt and pepper to taste and nutmeg. Stir in matzo meal. Batter should be quite thick but pourable.

☐ In a large frying pan, over high heat, heat 2 tablespoons oil. Drop batter by generous tablespoonsful into pan. Cook until undersides are lightly browned, about 2 minutes, then turn over and cook 2 minutes longer. Remove to paper towels to drain; keep warm. Continue until all batter is used, adding more oil to frying pan as needed. (Keep warm in a 150°C/300°F/Gas Mark 2 oven until all batter is used.) Serve hot with yogurt, sour cream or cream cheese, garnished with coriander or dill.

Poultry and Meat Dishes

Spiced Roast Chicken with Matzo Stuffing

Roast Goose with Fruity Stuffing

Spicy Barbecued Chicken

Chicken with Walnuts and Pomegranates

Israeli Roast Duck

North African-Style Poussins

Cochin-style Chilli Chicken

Spicy Turkey Schnitzel

Indian-Jewish Chicken

Seniyeh

Beef Tongue with Sweet-and-Sour Sauce

Mexican Beef Tzimmes

Hamin

Sweet-and-Sour Stuffed Cabbage

Old-fashioned Pot Roast with Onion Gravy

Cholent

Shashlik

Stuffed Passover Lamb

SPICED ROAST CHICKEN WITH MATZO STUFFING

SERVES 4

My sister-in-law prepares this matzo stuffing during Passover, but I find it delicious enough to use any time. She does not flavour her chicken with cumin and turmeric, typical of Morocco, Tunisia and other Middle Eastern countries, but I think the combination is a great success.

MATZO STUFFING

- 2 to 3 matzos, broken into small pieces
- 125 ml/4 fl oz chicken soup, stock or water, heated
- 1 tablespoon olive or vegetable oil
- 1 large onion, chopped
- 2 stalks celery, finely chopped
- Salt
- Freshly ground black pepper
- ½ teaspoon ground cumin (optional)
- ¼ teaspoon turmeric (optional)
- 1 tablespoon chopped fresh parsley
- 1 egg, beaten

- 1.6 to 1.8 kg/3½ to 4 lb roasting chicken
- 1 lemon, cut in half
- Salt
- Freshly ground black pepper
- 1 teaspoon ground cumin
- ¼ teaspoon ground turmeric
- 1 tablespoon olive oil
- 1 onion, thinly sliced
- Fresh parsley sprigs for garnish

☐ Prepare stuffing. Into a large bowl, place broken matzos. Pour hot chicken soup, stock or water over them and leave to stand until liquid is absorbed.

☐ In a large frying pan, over medium heat, heat oil. Add onion and celery and cook until vegetables begin to soften, 3 to 4 minutes. Add salt and pepper to taste and sprinkle in the cumin and turmeric, if using. Cook, stirring frequently, until mixture is golden, 4 to 5 minutes. Stir in matzo mixture. Remove from heat and leave to cool. Stir in chopped parsley and beaten egg.

☐ Preheat oven to 200°C/400°F/Gas Mark 6. Remove any excess fat from chicken and cavity. Wash under cold running water and pat dry with paper towels. Rub outside of chicken all over with lemon half; squeeze other half into cavity. Season chicken with salt and pepper to taste and cumin and turmeric. Rub or brush olive oil over.

☐ Spoon stuffing into bird and close with skewers or toothpicks if necessary. Place sliced onion in a medium roasting tin and lay the chicken on top. Roast, basting with the juices occasionally, for 1¼ to 1½ hours. Halfway through roasting time, add 125 to 250 ml/4 to 8 fl oz water to dissolve juices. Chicken is cooked through when juices run clear when leg is pierced with a knife or skewer.

☐ Transfer chicken to carving board and cover loosely with foil. Leave to rest in a warm place for 10 to 15 minutes.

☐ Pour any meat juices and onion into a small saucepan. Heat to boiling and reduce slightly, skimming any foam which comes to the surface. Pour into a gravy boat. Place chicken on serving platter, garnished with parsley. If you like, remove stuffing to a separate bowl for easier serving.

Roast Goose with Fruity Stuffing

SERVES 6 TO 8

Goose was so important in 16th-century Jewish cooking that it was known as the "Jew's fowl" in Germany: not only was the meat eaten, the fat rendered and used as the staple cooking fat, but the quills and down were sold and the liver used for liver pâté. Today, Israel is one of the world's main producers of geese and goose liver. In Northern European countries, goose is often roasted stuffed with apples or an apple-based stuffing. This fruity stuffing can be baked in a dish alongside the goose if you prefer; roast potatoes (in goose fat, of course!) make the perfect accompaniment.

- 3.6 to 4.5 kg/8 to 10 lb young goose, thawed if frozen
- Salt
- Freshly ground black pepper
- 1 tablespoon vegetable oil
- 1 large onion, chopped
- 6 to 8 tart apples, peeled, cored and cut up
- 90 g/3 oz raisins
- 215 g/7 oz prunes, chopped
- 100 g/3½ oz dried apricots, chopped
- 1 425 g/14 oz can cooked peeled chestnuts packed in water, drained
- ½ teaspoon crumbled dried sage
- 1 tablespoon chopped fresh parsley
- 1 tablespoon arrowroot
- 125 ml/4 fl oz apple juice
- 1 tablespoon cider vinegar
- Watercress and apple slices for garnish

☐ Remove all excess fat from inside and outside goose (discard or render for cooking fat). Cut off fatty skin flap near tail. Rub skin and sprinkle cavity with salt and pepper. Prick skin all over with a fork to let fat escape during roasting.

☐ In a large frying pan, over medium-high heat, heat vegetable oil. Add onion and cook until softened, 4 to 5 minutes. Add apples, raisins, prunes, apricots and chestnuts and sprinkle with sage and parsley. Stir in 2 tablespoons water and cook just until liquid evaporates, 2 to 3 minutes. Remove from heat and cool slightly.

☐ Preheat oven to 230°C/450°F/Gas Mark 8. Spoon stuffing into goose cavity and close with skewers or sew with kitchen string. Place goose on its back in a roasting tin and roast 30 minutes.

☐ Reduce oven to 180°C/350°F/Gas Mark 4. Remove goose from oven, pour off any fat and prick goose all over again. Turn goose on to its breast and roast for 1½ hours longer, removing fat from the tin and basting 3 or 4 more times. When no more fat is being released, add 250 ml/8 fl oz water to roasting tin and continue roasting until goose is done; juices should run slightly yellow or clear when leg is pierced with a skewer.

☐ When goose is done, remove to a serving platter; cover with foil and leave to rest 20 minutes in a warm place.

☐ Pour off all but 1 tablespoon fat from the tin drippings. Stir arrowroot, apple juice and vinegar together and add to tin with 125 ml/4 fl oz water, adding more water if necessary. Season with salt and pepper to taste. Bring to a boil, stirring and scraping up any bits from the tin. Reduce heat and simmer 5 minutes. Strain into a gravy boat. Arrange watercress and sliced apples around the goose and serve gravy separately.

BELOW SHABBAT CHICKEN, ARGENTINIAN-STYLE.

Spicy Barbecued Chicken

SERVES 6 TO 8

Barbecued foods are even more popular in Israel than the United States and the variety is amazing. No street corner is without an open fire covered with skewers of meat, chicken, chicken hearts and vegetables and patties of all kinds. Try this easy recipe using chicken. Serve with lots of potato salad and Israeli Salad (see pages 91 and 89).

- 1.8 to 2.25 kg/4 to 5 lb chicken portions
- 2 tablespoons olive oil
- 2 tablespoons ground cumin
- 1½ teaspoons turmeric
- 1 teaspoon hot or mild paprika or chilli powder
- Fresh coriander leaves for garnish

☐ Rub chicken portions with olive oil. Arrange on a baking sheet and sprinkle spices equally over both sides. Leave to stand while preparing a barbecue.

☐ Position barbecue rack about 12.5 cm/5 in above preheated coals. Arrange any legs and thighs on rack and cook 10 minutes. Add any breast portions to rack and cook 7 to 10 minutes longer. Raise rack if chicken browns too quickly.

☐ Turn chicken portions over and cook breasts 7 to 10 minutes longer and legs and thighs 12 to 15 minutes longer, or until juices run clear when chicken is pierced with a knife or skewer.

☐ Arrange chicken on a large serving platter and garnish with coriander leaves.

COOK'S TIP

LAMB CUBES CAN BE COOKED THE SAME WAY.

CHICKEN WITH WALNUTS AND POMEGRANATES

SERVES 4

Pomegranates are one of the most symbolic fruits in Jewish history. They are significant for Rosh Hashana, the New Year, and some Jewish communities even use pomegranate seeds in their Passover haroset. This braised chicken with walnuts and pomegranates is one of the most prized dishes among Iranian Jews. Serve with Chelou, a Persian-style rice (see page 86).

- 1 1.6 to 1.8 kg/3½ to 4 lb roasting chicken
- Salt
- Freshly ground black pepper
- 2 tablespoons vegetable oil
- 1 onion, finely chopped
- 275 g/9 oz walnuts, ground or finely chopped
- 450 ml/¾ pt pomegranate juice, or 125 ml/4 fl oz syrup diluted with 375 ml/12 fl oz water
- 2 tablespoons lemon juice
- 75 ml/2½ fl oz boiling water
- 1 tablespoon tomato paste
- 2 cinnamon sticks
- 2 tablespoons light brown sugar
- Watercress, pomegranate seeds and walnut halves for garnish

NOTE

POMEGRANATE JUICE IS AVAILABLE IN MIDDLE EASTERN FOOD SHOPS.

☐ Rinse chicken under cold running water and dry inside and out with paper towels. Season skin and cavity with salt and pepper.

☐ In a large casserole or heavy deep frying pan, over medium-high heat, heat oil. Add chicken and cook until golden brown, turning frequently to allow all sides to brown, 10 to 15 minutes. Remove to a large plate and set aside.

☐ Into pan, stir onion. Cook until beginning to soften, 2 to 3 minutes. Stir in ground or chopped walnuts and cook until well browned, 2 to 3 minutes. Pour in pomegranate juice or syrup mixture, lemon juice and boiling water. Stir in tomato paste, cinnamon sticks and brown sugar and bring just to a boil. Reduce heat to low.

☐ Return chicken to pan and cook, covered, until chicken is tender and juices run clear when leg is pierced with a knife or skewer, 45 to 50 minutes. Remove chicken to a serving platter and cover with foil to keep warm. If sauce is too thin, bring sauce up to a boil and reduce until thickened slightly.

☐ Pour sauce over chicken, garnish platter with watercress and pomegranate seeds and arrange walnut halves over top.

BELOW TRADITIONAL METHODS OF FARMING STILL EXIST IN ISRAEL, PRACTISED MAINLY BY ARABS.

ISRAELI ROAST DUCK

SERVES 4

New breeds of duck are being bred in Israel for both eating and for the production of foie gras for liver pâté. The combination of orange and sugar makes a lovely glaze, but grapefruit juice can also be used. A simple gravy can be served with the duck, or it can be served with apple sauce and Latkes (see page 73).

- 2.25 kg to 2.7 kg/5 to 6 lb duckling, thawed if frozen
- Salt
- Freshly ground black pepper
- ½ orange, quartered
- 1 tablespoon light brown sugar
- 175 ml/6 fl oz fresh orange juice
- 1 onion, thinly sliced
- 1 carrot, thinly sliced
- 1 tablespoon plain flour
- 175 ml/6 fl oz chicken stock or water
- 1 tablespoon cider or distilled white vinegar
- 1 tablespoon orange marmalade
- Fresh parsley sprigs for garnish

☐ Rinse the duck under cold running water. Pat it dry inside and out with paper towels. Remove any excess fat from outside or inside the cavity. Sprinkle cavity with salt and pepper and rub skin with salt and pepper. Prick skin all over with a fork to let fat escape. Place orange quarters in cavity.

☐ In a small bowl, mix brown sugar and 1 teaspoon salt with 3 to 4 tablespoons orange juice. Reserve remaining juice.

☐ Preheat oven to 180°C/350°F/Gas Mark 4. Place the sliced onion and carrot into roasting tin; place duck on a rack on top. Roast duck 30 minutes. Remove from oven and baste duck. Pour off fat and prick skin all over again.

☐ Continue roasting duck, basting it and pouring off fat every 20 minutes, until duck is well browned and skin is crisp, 1½ hours. The juices should run clear when upper leg is pierced with a sharp knife or skewer.

☐ Remove duck to a serving platter, cover with foil and leave to stand 15 minutes.

☐ Pour off all but 1 tablespoon fat from tin. Stir in flour. Cook, stirring and scraping the dripping from the tin, 1 to 2 minutes. Stir in remaining orange juice, chicken stock or water, cider or vinegar and marmalade. Bring to a boil and simmer until well blended and thickened, 3 to 4 minutes.

☐ Pour gravy into a gravy boat and serve separately. Garnish duck with parsley and serve quartered or carve at the table.

NORTH AFRICAN-STYLE POUSSINS

SERVES 4

Couscous is a popular grain in Morocco and Tunisia and makes an ideal base for a poultry stuffing. Here it is combined with typical North African spices and used to stuff the popular poussin. It can be used to stuff a whole chicken or baked on its own.

- 4 tablespoons olive oil
- 1 small onion, finely chopped
- 2 garlic cloves, peeled and finely chopped
- 2 cm/¾ in piece fresh ginger root, finely chopped
- 60 g/2 oz pecan halves, toasted and coarsely chopped
- 250 g/8 oz quick-cooking couscous
- Salt
- Freshly ground black pepper
- ½ teaspoon cinnamon
- 60 g/2 oz sultanas
- 100 g/3½ oz no-soak dried apricots, chopped
- 4 tablespoons chopped fresh mint, or 1 tablespoon dried
- 250 ml/8 fl oz tomato juice
- 250 ml/8 fl oz boiling water
- 4 poussins
- ½ teaspoon ground ginger
- ½ teaspoon hot paprika
- Fresh parsley sprigs or watercress for garnish

☐ In a large frying pan, over medium-high heat, heat 2 tablespoons olive oil. Add onion and cook 2 to 3 minutes. Stir in garlic and ginger root and cook 1 minute longer; add pecans and stir.

☐ Add couscous with salt and pepper to taste, cinnamon, sultanas, apricots and mint. Stir well to blend. Pour in the tomato juice and water, shaking pan to distribute ingredients evenly. Remove from heat and leave to stand 5 minutes. Remove lid and fluff stuffing mixture with a fork. Cool and taste for seasoning.

☐ Preheat oven to 190°C/375°F/Gas Mark 5. Rinse birds under cold running water and pat dry with paper towels. Rub birds with remaining olive oil; sprinkle cavity with salt and pepper and rub ginger and paprika into the skin.

☐ Spoon about 60 to 75 g/2 to 3 oz stuffing mixture into each bird and tie legs with string. Cover remaining stuffing mixture loosely and set aside. Lightly grease a large roasting tin and arrange birds in tin.

☐ Roast birds until crisp and golden and juices run clear when a leg is pierced with a knife or skewer, about 1 hour.

☐ Remove poussins to a serving platter and cover with foil. Add 60 ml/2 fl oz water to roasting tin and stir, scraping up any bits on bottom of tin. Uncover remaining couscous mixture and pour in juices from tin. Reheat couscous mixture over medium-low heat 2 to 3 minutes, stirring and fluffing with a fork. Spoon into a serving dish and garnish with a few parsley sprigs or watercress. Serve poussins garnished with parsley or watercress.

BELOW FRESH, SUCCULENT FRUIT IS AN IMPORTANT PART OF THE TYPICAL LEVANTINE DIET.

Cochin-Style Chilli Chicken

SERVES 4

This recipe is based on a dish which comes from the Jewish community in Cochin, in southern India. I have toned down the "heat" somewhat as the original quantity of chillies would be too strong for the average taste. This makes a change from the ordinary braised chicken dish and, as it can be kept warm, makes an ideal choice for a Friday night supper, which is when it is often served in Cochin. Hot boiled rice is the ideal accompaniment.

- 2 tablespoons lemon juice
- 1 teaspoon salt
- 2 tablespoons sugar
- 2 tablespoons vegetable oil
- 10 to 12 fresh or dried curry leaves, or 1 teaspoon curry powder
- 375 g/12 oz shallots, sliced
- 6 garlic cloves, finely chopped
- 2.5 cm/1 in piece fresh ginger root, finely chopped
- 5 medium-hot green chillies, seeded and very finely sliced
- 2 medium tomatoes, chopped
- ½ teaspoon turmeric
- ¼ teaspoon chilli powder
- 1 1.4 to 1.6 kg/3 to 3½ lb chicken, jointed into 8
- 2 tablespoons chopped fresh coriander
- Fresh coriander leaves and lemon wedges for garnish

☐ In a small bowl, place lemon juice, ¼ teaspoon salt and sugar; stir to dissolve. Set aside.

☐ In a casserole or large deep frying pan, over medium-high heat, heat oil. Add curry leaves or curry powder and stir until they sizzle, 10 to 15 seconds. Stir in shallots, garlic, ginger, and chillies and cook until the shallots have softened and begin to colour, 5 to 7 minutes. Stir in tomatoes, turmeric, chilli powder and remaining salt. Cook 3 to 4 minutes longer.

☐ Add chicken to vegetable mixture, moving pieces around to cover with some vegetables. Stir in 250 ml/8 fl oz water and bring just to a boil. Reduce heat to low and cook, covered tightly, 20 minutes, stirring once.

☐ Uncover and stir in reserved lemon-juice mixture and chopped coriander. Increase heat to medium and cook, uncovered, until sauce is slightly reduced, basting chicken occasionally with the sauce, about 10 minutes.

☐ Arrange chicken pieces on a serving platter. Pour sauce over and garnish with coriander leaves and lemon wedges.

SPICY TURKEY SCHNITZEL

SERVES 4

Israel produces great quantities of turkey and chicken and prepares it in ways usually used for other meats, unavailable or too costly. Veal would be prohibitively expensive, so the old-fashioned veal dish of Wiener schnitzel is made with turkey breast and popular Israeli spices. This is one of the most popular dishes in Israel.

- 625 g/1¼ lb turkey breast, cut into 8 slices about 1.25 cm/½ in thick
- 1 teaspoon ground cumin
- ½ teaspoon turmeric
- ½ teaspoon hot paprika
- ½ teaspoon salt
- Freshly ground black pepper
- ⅛ teaspoon cayenne pepper or chilli powder
- 60 g/2 oz plain flour
- 2 eggs, beaten
- 125 g/4 oz matzo meal, or fine fresh breadcrumbs
- Vegetable oil for frying
- Lemon wedges and fresh parsley sprigs for garnish

☐ Place each turkey slice between 2 sheets greaseproof paper and pound them to flatten as thin as possible.

☐ In a small bowl, combine cumin, turmeric, paprika, salt, pepper to taste and cayenne pepper or chilli powder. Rub spice mixture onto turkey slices and leave 30 minutes.

☐ Into 3 pie plates or shallow dishes, place flour, beaten eggs and matzo meal or breadcrumbs. Dip each spice-covered turkey slice first into flour to coat, shaking off the excess; then into the egg, brushing to coat completely; then into matzo meal or crumbs. Arrange on a baking sheet.

☐ In a large frying pan or on a griddle, over medium-high heat, heat 2 to 3 tablespoons oil. Add a few turkey slices, but do not allow to overlap. Fry quickly, until underside is golden brown, about 2 minutes, then, using a fish slice, carefully turn slices over. Cook until other side is browned and turkey cooked, 1 to 2 minutes longer. Continue to cook in batches, adding more oil if necessary. Remove to paper towels to drain.

☐ Arrange turkey slices on an ovenproof serving platter and keep warm while cooking remaining slices. Garnish turkey schnitzel with lemon wedges and parsley sprigs.

INDIAN-JEWISH CHICKEN

SERVES 4

This is a very aromatic dish, often served in the Bene Israel community of Bombay. It is an ideal Sabbath dish and can easily be prepared and cooked overnight in a slow cooker or very low oven.

- 1.4 to 1.6 kg/3 to 3½ lb chicken
- 125 ml/4 fl oz vegetable oil
- Salt
- Freshly ground black pepper
- 1 onion, cut in half and thinly sliced
- 2 garlic cloves, finely chopped
- 2 bay leaves
- 1 cinnamon stick
- 4 whole cloves
- 4 cardamom pods
- 1 tablespoon curry powder or garam masala
- 1 tablespoon finely chopped or grated ginger root
- ¼ teaspoon turmeric
- 250 ml/8 fl oz chicken or vegetable stock or water
- Fresh parsley sprigs for garnish

☐ Rinse chicken under cold running water and pat dry with paper towels. On a cutting board, remove legs and thighs from body and separate drumstick from thigh. Remove wing tips; remove breasts and wings from carcass and cut each breast into 2 pieces; upper breast portion can include wing. This gives you 8 pieces. (Wing tips and carcass can be used for soup.)

☐ Preheat oven to 130°C/250°F/Gas Mark ½. In a large casserole or deep frying pan with ovenproof lid, over medium-high heat, heat oil. Add chicken pieces, season with salt and pepper and cook until underside is golden, 5 to 7 minutes. Turn chicken pieces and add remaining ingredients, stirring well.

☐ Cover pan tightly and bake, basting occasionally, for 1½ to 2 hours, adding a little more chicken stock or water if all liquid has been absorbed.

☐ To serve, arrange the chicken pieces on a serving platter and pour any juices over; garnish with parsley sprigs.

ABOVE Spicy Turkey Schnitzel.

SENIYEH

SERVES 4 TO 6

This traditional Yemenite dish is a kosher version of moussaka, a Greek speciality. Replacing the milk-based béchamel sauce with a tahini topping makes this a great Sabbath supper dish. Serve with mashed potatoes or lots of rice and salad.

- 500 g/1 lb lean minced lamb
- 1 tablespoon plain flour
- 2 onions, finely chopped
- 2 garlic cloves, peeled and finely chopped
- 2 tablespoons chopped fresh parsley or coriander
- ½ teaspoon ground cinnamon
- Salt
- Freshly ground black pepper
- ½ teaspoon zhoug (see page 11), or ¼ teaspoon cayenne pepper
- 2 tablespoons olive oil
- 30 g/1 oz pine nuts, toasted
- 125 ml/8 fl oz tahini
- 3 to 4 tablespoons lemon juice

☐ Into a large bowl, place meat. Sprinkle with flour and toss to mix. Add onions, garlic, parsley or coriander and cinnamon and mix well. Season with salt and pepper to taste. Stir in the zhoug or cayenne, oil and 2 tablespoons pine nuts.

☐ Preheat oven to 180°C/350°F/Gas Mark 4. Lightly oil a shallow 2 l/3¼ pt round baking dish. Spread meat mixture in dish, smoothing top evenly.

☐ In a small bowl, mix tahini, lemon juice and 1 to 2 tablespoons water. Pour over meat mixture and sprinkle with remaining pine nuts.

☐ Cook, uncovered, until top is brown and bubbling and meat is cooked, 35 to 40 minutes. (Knife or skewer should feel hot when inserted into centre of meat, held for 30 seconds and then removed.)

BEEF TONGUE WITH SWEET-AND-SOUR SAUCE

SERVES 6 TO 8

Tongue has had a special symbolism for Jews since Biblical times, when Abraham prepared a feast for the angels, choosing tongue as one of the gifts. The sweet-and-sour version, particularly popular with German and Polish Jews, is traditional at Sukkot. This is my mother's recipe.

- 1 1.8 kg/4 lb beef tongue
- 1 tablespoon distilled white vinegar
- 6 whole cloves
- 1 tablespoon black peppercorns
- 1 bay leaf
- Fresh parsley sprigs for garnish

SWEET-AND-SOUR SAUCE

- 1 tablespoon chicken fat or vegetable oil
- 2 onions, thinly sliced
- 1 tablespoon plain flour
- ½ teaspoon salt
- Freshly ground black pepper
- 1 cinnamon stick
- 3 to 4 whole cloves
- 125 ml/4 fl oz tomato sauce
- Grated zest and juice of 1 lemon
- 3 tablespoons light brown sugar
- 1 tablespoon honey
- 90 g/3 oz raisins

COOK'S TIP

PICKLED OR SMOKED TONGUE CAN BE USED FOR THE SAME RECIPE, BUT THE TONGUE SHOULD BE SOAKED FOR SEVERAL HOURS OR OVERNIGHT IN SEVERAL CHANGES OF COLD WATER BEFORE COOKING. OMIT ANY ADDITIONAL SALT IF USING PICKLED OR SMOKED TONGUE.

☐ Into a large stockpot or saucepan, place tongue, vinegar, cloves, peppercorns and bay leaf. Cover with cold water and, over high heat, bring to a boil. Skim off any foam which comes to the surface. Boil, skimming often, 5 minutes. Reduce heat to medium-low and simmer until tongue is tender when pierced with a fork, 3 to 4 hours. Add a little water from time to time if necessary to keep tongue covered with liquid.

☐ Remove from heat, but leave tongue to cool in its cooking liquid. When cool, remove tongue from liquid. With a sharp knife, peel off outer skin and the gristle at back of tongue. Set tongue aside. Reserve cooking liquid.

☐ Make sauce. In a large, deep pan, over medium heat, heat chicken fat or oil. Add onions and cook until soft and beginning to colour, 5 to 7 minutes. Sprinkle onions with flour and cook, stirring constantly, until flour is browned, 1 minute. Slowly add about 450 ml/¾ pt reserved cooking liquid and cook, stirring constantly, until smooth and slightly thickened, about 2 minutes.

☐ Add salt and pepper to taste, then stir in remaining ingredients. Reduce heat to medium-low and simmer, stirring often, 10 minutes. Remove cinnamon stick and cloves.

☐ Slice tongue into 6 mm/¼ in slices and add to sauce. Cook until tongue is heated though, 2 to 3 minutes. Arrange tongue slices on a serving platter or directly on individual dinner plates and spoon over a little sauce. Garnish with parsley sprigs.

ABOVE MOROCCAN JEWS STUDYING THE TORAH (THE FIVE BOOKS OF MOSES).

MEXICAN BEEF TZIMMES

SERVES 8

A Jewish-Mexican family with whom I once spent a summer in Mexico City had an elderly German-Jewish cook. This is her version of German tzimmes. It combines old-world tradition with new-world ingredients.

Tzimmes is a slowly cooked casserole of meat, sweet vegetables, such as carrots or sweet potatoes, and fruit, most often prunes.

- 1.6 kg/3½ lb boneless beef brisket
- 1½ tablespoons plain flour
- 4 to 6 tablespoons chicken fat *or* vegetable oil
- 2 onions, thinly sliced
- 2 to 4 garlic cloves, peeled
- 2 425 g/14 oz cans tomatoes
- 1 large mango, peeled and flesh puréed
- 1 teaspoon salt
- ½ teaspoon dried red-pepper flakes, or to taste
- 1 teaspoon chilli powder
- 1 cinnamon stick
- 2 bay leaves
- 4 tablespoons honey
- 4 carrots, sliced
- 2 large sweet potatoes or yams, peeled and cut into chunks
- 215 g/7 oz pitted prunes, soaked in hot water for 2 hours and well drained
- 2 425 g/14 oz cans red kidney beans, rinsed and drained
- 4 tablespoons chopped fresh coriander

☐ Rinse beef under cold running water; dry well with paper towels. Dredge meat with flour on both sides.

☐ In a large casserole with tight-fitting lid, over medium-high heat, heat 2 to 3 tablespoons chicken fat or oil. Add beef and cook until underside is well browned, 5 to 7 minutes, turn beef and cook until second side is well browned, 4 to 5 minutes longer. Remove to a plate and set aside.

☐ Add remaining chicken fat or oil and onions. Cook until onion is softened and beginning to colour, 3 to 5 minutes. Stir in garlic and cook 1 minute longer. Pour in tomatoes and their juice, stirring to break up tomatoes and scrape up any meat juices. Add mango purée, salt, red-pepper flakes, chilli powder, cinnamon stick, bay leaves and honey and cook, stirring often, 2 to 3 minutes.

☐ Return beef to casserole and pour in enough water to just cover meat. Cover tightly and simmer, over medium-low heat, 1½ hours. (Check from time to time to see if there is enough water.) Add carrots, sweet potato chunks, prunes and beans. Cover and cook, over medium heat, 30 minutes longer, adding a little more water if necessary.

☐ Remove meat to a deep serving platter. If liquid is too thin, reduce over medium-high heat until slightly thickened, 5 to 10 minutes. Spoon vegetables and beans around beef. Pour sauce over meat and sprinkle meat and vegetables with chopped coriander. Serve meat cut into thin slices.

ABOVE COLORFUL DECORATION ON BOATS IN THE HODEIDAH FISH MARKET IN YEMEN.

HAMIN

SERVES 8

Hamin, from the Hebrew for cholent, is the Sephardic version of the same slowly cooked stew. The Iranians, Afghanis and Kurds use quinces and flower-scented waters, especially rosewater, in their cooking, and this recipe uses both. Originally dried rose buds or rose petals were used, but rosewater is more easily available at Greek and Middle Eastern grocery shops. These flavours provide a more exotic and highly perfumed dish which can be made with chicken, beef or, as used in this recipe, lamb.

- 2 tablespoons vegetable oil
- 2 onions, thinly sliced
- 4 garlic cloves, finely chopped
- 2.25 to 2.7 kg/5 to 6 lb shoulder of lamb, boned, trimmed of fat and cut into large cubes
- 4 potatoes, peeled and sliced
- 4 carrots, thinly sliced
- 500 g/1 lb pumpkin or butternut squash, peeled and cut into cubes
- 625 g/1¼ lb basmati or other long-grain rice, rinsed and drained
- 500 g/1 lb quinces, peeled, quartered, cored and sliced
- 1 cinnamon stick
- 4 whole cloves
- 2 teaspoons salt
- Freshly ground black pepper
- 1 tablespoon rosewater (optional)
- 2 eggs, lightly beaten

COOK'S TIP

As lamb may contain additional fat, it is desirable to prepare this 2 days ahead. Leave to cool, then refrigerate. When cold, scrape off any fat from surface and reheat in a 180°C/350°F/Gas Mark 4 oven

☐ In a large ovenproof casserole with tight-fitting lid, over medium- high heat, heat oil. Add onions and cook until just golden, 5 to 7 minutes. Stir in garlic and cook 1 minute longer. Remove to plate and set aside.

☐ Into same casserole, add meat and cook on all sides until pieces are well browned, 7 to 10 minutes. You may need to cook in batches – do not crowd pan. Remove meat to another plate and remove casserole from heat, leaving any remaining oil.

☐ Preheat oven to 230°C/450°F/Gas Mark 8. Cover bottom of the casserole with potato slices, spreading them evenly. Add carrots in one layer and then pumpkin cubes. Add rice and meat. Cover meat with onion-garlic mixture, spreading to cover meat. Top with quince slices, cinnamon stick and cloves and sprinkle with salt and pepper to taste. Sprinkle with rosewater if using.

☐ Mix eggs with 250 ml/8 fl oz water and pour into pan with enough cold water to cover the ingredients. Cook for 30 minutes, then reduce heat to lowest setting, around 100°C/200°F/Gas Mark ¼, and continue cooking 8 to 10 hours or overnight. Serve the hamin from casserole.

ABOVE Children offering the first fruits for *Shavuot* (Feast of Weeks) also known as the Festival of Fruits.

SWEET-AND-SOUR STUFFED CABBAGE

SERVES 6 TO 8

There are many versions of this traditional Sukkot dish in the Eastern-European Jewish tradition, with as many names. *Goluptsy*, as it is called in Russia, is made with a sweet-and-sour tomato-based sauce. In other countries, such as Hungary, it is not. This is the recipe my aunt used to prepare for my father. He loved it served with mashed potatoes.

- 1 large cabbage
- 30 g/1 oz dried seasoned breadcrumbs
- 125 ml/4 fl oz vegetable stock or water
- 1 tablespoon vegetable oil
- 1 onion, finely chopped
- 2 garlic cloves, peeled and finely chopped
- 1 kg/2 lb minced beef
- ¾ teaspoon salt
- Freshly ground black pepper
- 4 tablespoons tomato ketchup
- 2 eggs, beaten
- 2 to 3 tablespoons chopped fresh dill
- 100 g/3½ oz long-grain rice
- Chopped fresh dill for garnish

SAUCE

- 2 425 g/14 oz cans tomatoes
- 450 ml/¾ pt tomato sauce
- 8 tablespoons tomato ketchup
- Salt
- Freshly ground pepper
- 2 onions, thinly sliced
- Grated zest and juice of 1 lemon
- 75 g/2½ oz light brown sugar
- 125 g/4 oz sultanas

ABOVE A POIGNANT REMINDER OF THE JEWISH COMMUNITY ON THIS HOUSE IN THE OLD QUARTER OF KRAKOW, POLAND.

☐ Core centre out of cabbage and gently remove as many leaves as possible; smaller leaves can be overlapped to form a large leaf. Bring a large saucepan of water to a boil. Plunge in leaves (it may be necessary to do this in batches) and simmer until the leaves are softened, but not cooked tender, 3–5 minutes. Drain into a colander and rinse under cold running water; set aside.

☐ In a small bowl, combine breadcrumbs and vegetable stock or water and leave to stand until liquid is absorbed.

☐ In a small frying pan, over medium-high heat, heat oil. Add onion and cook until onion is softened and beginning to colour, 3 to 5 minutes. Add garlic and cook 1 minute longer, stirring occasionally. Remove from heat and set aside.

☐ In a large bowl, with a fork, mix beef, salt and pepper to taste, ketchup, eggs, chopped dill and rice. Stir in breadcrumbs and cooked onions; mix until very well blended.

☐ In a shallow roasting tin with tight-fitting lid, combine all sauce ingredients. Over medium-high heat, bring to a boil, then reduce heat and simmer, stirring occasionally, 15 to 20 minutes.

☐ Preheat oven to 170°C/325°F/Gas Mark 3. Arrange a cabbage leaf on a flat work surface, remove any heavy core from leaf if necessary. Place 1 to 2 tablespoons meat mixture (exact amount will depend on the size of the leaf) in centre of each cabbage leaf. Fold sides over stuffing, then roll cabbage leaf jelly-roll fashion to completely enclose the stuffing. Place on a baking sheet or tray and continue until all meat mixture is used. (Any leftover cabbage can be thinly shredded and added to the sauce.)

☐ Arrange all cabbage packages, seam-sides down, in the sauce-filled roasting tin and spoon some sauce over cabbage packages. Add a little water if necessary; cabbages should be *just* covered with liquid. Cover and cook about 1½ hours.

☐ Remove lid and baste cabbage packages with sauce. With a slotted spoon, remove packages to a deep serving plate and keep warm. If liquid is very thin, reduce over medium-high heat until slightly thickened. If it is too thick, add a little water; pour over cabbage and sprinkle with the chopped dill.

OLD-FASHIONED POT ROAST WITH ONION GRAVY

SERVES 8 TO 10

This typical Russian-Jewish dish has become a staple of the American-Jewish repertoire. There are many versions, probably the best known is the shortcut recipe made with a package of onion soup mix! This is just as easy and made with the real thing; it is best served with mashed potatoes.

- 1 2.25 to 2.7 kg/5 to 6 lb brisket of beef or boneless beef shoulder
- 1 tablespoon plain flour
- 4 tablespoons vegetable oil
- 6 onions, cut into 1.25 cm/ ½ in rings
- 4 to 6 garlic cloves, peeled and finely chopped
- 250 ml/8 fl oz tomato juice
- Salt
- Freshly ground black pepper
- ½ teaspoon dried thyme
- ½ teaspoon paprika
- 1 bay leaf
- 6 carrots, cut into 6 mm/¼ in slices on the diagonal
- Fresh parsley sprigs to garnish

COOK'S TIP

AS WITH ALL SLOWLY COOKED STEWS AND MEATS, THIS DISH IS BEST COOKED A DAY AHEAD. REFRIGERATE AND SKIM OFF CONGEALED FAT. REHEAT IN A 180°C/350°F/GAS MARK 4 OVEN FOR 35 TO 40 MINUTES.

☐ Rinse meat under cold running water; pat dry with paper towels. Trim any visible fat, then dust meat with flour.

☐ In a large ovenproof casserole, over medium-high heat, heat 2 tablespoons oil. Add meat and cook until browned on underside, 5 to 7 minutes. Turn meat and cook until other side is browned, 5 to 6 minutes longer. Remove to a plate.

☐ Preheat oven to 170°C/325°F/Gas Mark 3. Add remaining oil to casserole and stir in onions. Cook until onions begin to soften and colour, 4 to 5 minutes. Add garlic and cook 1 minute longer. Pour in tomato juice, stirring and scraping to pick up any bits from bottom. Season with salt and pepper to taste, thyme, paprika and bay leaf.

☐ Return beef to pan and add enough water to cover all ingredients. Bring to a boil and skim off any foam that comes to the surface. Cover tightly and cook in the oven until beef is fork-tender, 3 to 3½ hours. Add carrots to pot and cook until tender, 30 minutes longer.

☐ Remove casserole from the oven and remove lid. If liquid is too thin, remove the beef to a deep serving platter and reduce gravy to thicken slightly. Spoon gravy with onions and carrots around beef and garnish with parsley. Serve meat carved into 6 mm/¼ in slices.

Cholent

SERVES 8 TO 10

Cholent is a long-simmering stew cooked on Friday night and served at noon after the Sabbath morning service. It has probably been made since Biblical times and is found in all Jewish communities, but with slightly differing ingredients and flavourings; the essential ingredients being meat and beans. The key is the long, slow cooking to tenderize an economical cut of meat and that the stew can be left to cook for a long time at a low temperature.

A cholent, meaning "hot-slow" in French, is made by every Ashkenazic Jewish family and is really a layered hotpot that can include meat, chicken, beans, sausages, dumplings and potatoes. Its counterpart is found in the Sephardic dfina, which is prepared all over the Middle East. A hamin, from the Hebrew for cholent, is eaten by Jews along the Afghan border, as well as in Iran, Italy and Israel.

This is a typical Ashkenazic version and contains a special dumpling called a cholent knaidle.

- 2 tablespoons vegetable oil
- 4 onions, cut in half and sliced
- 4 garlic cloves, peeled and finely chopped
- 1.4 kg/3 lb boneless flank, brisket or beef shoulder, cut into large cubes
- 425 g/14 oz dried lima, haricot, or red kidney beans, soaked at least 8 hours
- 215 g/7 oz cup pot barley
- 10 to 12 medium potatoes, peeled and halved or, if large, quartered
- 2 teaspoons salt
- Freshly ground black pepper
- 1½ teaspoons dried thyme
- 1 teaspoon paprika
- 2 bay leaves
- 2 tablespoons sugar

CHOLENT KNAIDLE

- 175 g/6 oz plain flour
- ¾ teaspoon baking powder
- ½ teaspoon salt
- Freshly ground black pepper
- 175 g/6 oz chicken fat or chicken flavoured vegetable fat
- 2 tablespoons chopped fresh parsley

☐ In a large ovenproof casserole with tight-fitting lid, over medium-high heat, heat oil. Add onions and cook until well browned, 7 to 10 minutes. Stir in garlic and cook 1 minute longer. Remove to a plate and set aside.

☐ Into same casserole, add meat and cook on all sides until pieces are well browned, 7 to 10 minutes. You may need to cook in batches – do not crowd pan. Remove meat to another plate and remove casserole from heat, leaving any remaining oil.

☐ Return onions and garlic to casserole, spreading them evenly over bottom. Drain beans and add them, then layer in beef cubes, barley and potatoes, sprinkling salt, pepper to taste, thyme and paprika between layers. Tuck in bay leaves.

☐ In a small saucepan, over high heat, bring sugar to a boil with 2 tablespoons water. Cook until sugar turns a dark caramel colour, 1 to 2 minutes. Off the heat and holding pan away from you, carefully pour in 60 ml/2 fl oz cold water (caramel will splatter). Return to heat to liquidize caramel, then pour into casserole.

☐ Pour in enough water to just cover meat, vegetables and bean layers and, over high heat, bring to a boil. Skim off any foam which comes to the surface. Lower heat slightly and cook 30 minutes, skimming occasionally. Add a little more water if necessary to be sure all ingredients are covered.

☐ Prepare knaidle. Preheat oven to 100°C/200°F/Gas Mark ¼ or lowest setting. Into a medium bowl, sift flour, baking powder, salt and pepper to taste. Cut in chicken fat or chicken-flavoured vegetable fat. Add chopped parsley and 4 to 6 tablespoons cold water, then stir to form a soft dough. Form into large dumpling or a sausage shape.

☐ Remove casserole from heat. Gently place knaidle on top of ingredients in the casserole, tucking it in gently. Cover tightly and cook in the very low oven 10 to 12 hours or overnight. Serve cholent from the casserole; slice the knaidle into serving pieces or serve separately.

SHASHLIK

SERVES 6

Shashlik, shish kabob and kebab are terms which mean lamb or beef grilled on a skewer. Skewered meat cooked over an open fire was probably one of the original ways of cooking meat. Traditional in the Russian republics, the Balkans and the Middle East, its modern form, the barbecue, is very popular in Israel and the United States. Israeli street food often features skewers of marinated cubed lamb, and many Russian-Jewish immigrants now sell shashlik beside the traditional hot dog men in New York City! Serve with rice and Israeli Salad (see page 89).

MARINADE

- 175 ml/6 fl oz cup olive oil
- 125 ml/4 fl oz lemon juice
- 125 ml/4 fl oz dry red wine or dry sherry
- 2 to 3 tablespoons chopped fresh rosemary, or 1 tablespoon dried
- ½ small onion, finely chopped or grated
- 4 to 6 garlic cloves, peeled and finely chopped
- 1 teaspoon salt
- Freshly ground black pepper
- ½ teaspoon red-pepper flakes (optional)
- 1.8 kg/4 lb boneless lamb shoulder, trimmed of all visible fat and cut into 5 cm/2 in cubes
- 4 small onions, root ends attached, cut into eighths
- 500 g/1 lb cherry tomatoes
- 2 yellow or red peppers, cored, seeded and cut into 2.5 cm/1 in squares
- Fresh rosemary sprigs for garnish

☐ In a large, shallow nonmetallic baking dish, combine marinade ingredients, stirring until well blended and creamy. Add lamb cubes and stir around until well coated. Cover and refrigerate 6 hours or overnight, stirring occasionally.

☐ Position barbecue rack about 12.5 cm/5 in above preheated coals.

☐ Thread lamb cubes on to metal skewers, leaving a small space between cubes so meat cooks evenly. Thread onion pieces, cherry tomatoes and pepper squares on to separate skewers; brush with some remaining marinade.

☐ Arrange lamb skewers over centre of coals and cook, turning and basting with marinade occasionally, 17 to 20 minutes. Halfway through cooking time, add vegetable skewers to barbecue and cook, turning and basting with marinade, 8 to 10 minutes.

☐ Arrange skewers on long serving platter and surround with fresh sprigs of rosemary. Serve with rice, Israeli Salad or other accompaniments.

ABOVE IT IS CUSTOMARY FOR JEWS TO GO TO THE WESTERN WALL IN JERUSALEM TO PRAY ON THE SABBATH.

STUFFED PASSOVER LAMB

SERVES 6 TO 8

Although some Jewish communities do not eat lamb at Passover, it is traditional throughout the Middle East and other lamb-producing countries, such as England. It is a popular choice for a Sephardic Passover Seder because young lamb is at its best in springtime. As with other meats, the hindquarters are not generally kosher, so the shoulder is preferable. Ask your butcher to bone the lamb and cut a pocket for the stuffing.

STUFFING

- 1 tablespoon olive or vegetable oil
- 1 onion, finely chopped
- 2 garlic cloves, peeled and finely chopped
- 250 g/8 oz lean minced lamb
- 100 g/3½ oz long-grain rice
- Salt
- Freshly ground black pepper
- ½ teaspoon ground cumin
- ⅛ teaspoon turmeric
- 1 tablespoon chopped fresh coriander
- 60 g/2 oz walnuts or almonds, chopped
- 90 g/3 oz raisins
- 100 g/3½ oz dried apricots, chopped
- 1 egg, beaten
- 1 1.8 to 2.25 kg/4 to 5 lb shoulder of lamb, boned, pocketed and trimmed of fat
- 2 tablespoons olive oil
- 2 tablespoons honey
- 2 tablespoons arrowroot
- 250 ml/8 fl oz beef or chicken stock
- 1 tablespoon cider vinegar
- Fresh watercress for garnish

☐ Prepare stuffing. In a medium frying pan over medium-high heat, heat oil. Add onion and cook until onion begins to soften and colour, 3 to 5 minutes. Stir in garlic and cook 1 minute longer.

☐ Add minced lamb and cook, stirring with a fork to break up meat, until meat is no longer pink, 4 to 5 minutes. Stir in rice and cook until rice turns golden and translucent, 5 minutes longer. Pour in 75 ml/2½ fl oz hot water, salt and pepper to taste, cumin and turmeric. Cook, covered, over medium-low heat, until rice is just tender and all liquid has been absorbed, 12 to 15 minutes. Remove from heat and cool slightly. Stir in coriander, nuts, raisins, apricots and beaten egg.

☐ Preheat oven to 180°C/350°F/Gas Mark 4. Lay meat on work surface, skin side down. Season with salt and pepper to taste and spread stuffing evenly over the meat to within 2.5 cm/1 in of edges. Roll up meat as neatly as possible and tie at 5 cm/2 in intervals with kitchen string. Rub surface of meat with olive oil and sprinkle with salt and pepper.

☐ Place meat, seam-side down, on a rack in a roasting tin. Roast for 20 minutes per pound for medium. About 20 minutes before meat is done, brush with the honey. Return to oven.

☐ Remove lamb to a serving platter, cover with foil, keep warm and leave to stand 15 minutes.

☐ Meanwhile, remove rack from tin and pour off all but about 2 tablespoons fat. Mix arrowroot with 60 ml/2 fl oz water and pour into tin with stock and vinegar. Bring to a boil, stirring often, and reduce heat to medium-low and simmer until smooth and slightly thickened, 7 to 10 minutes.

☐ Pour gravy into gravy boat to serve separately. Garnish lamb with watercress.

ABOVE NOTE THE *PEYOT* (SIDELOCKS) ON THESE TWO SEPHARDIC JEWS.

Fish Dishes

Gefilte Fish
Curried Fish Fillets
Baked Salmon with Avocado-Dill Sauce
Jewish-Style Fried Fish
Red Snapper with Green Sauce
Baked Trout with Pomegranate
Sweet-and-Sour Fish

GEFILTE FISH

SERVES 6

The title gefilte fish comes from the German for "filled fish". Originally, skinned and boned fish was stuffed with a minced fish mixture and slowly simmered. After chilling, the rich stock became jellied and was served as part of the dish or separately. Nowadays, however, the mixture is generally formed into balls and simmered in stock. It is also very attractive when packed into a ring mould and baked in the oven, or even microwaved! Of course, cooked in this way there is no jelly as an accompaniment.

Although freshwater carp and pike were traditional for making gefilte fish, most cooks prefer a mixture of saltwater white fish. But whatever fish you use, gefilte fish is always served with carrot slices and beetroot-flavoured horseradish sauce!

FISH STOCK

- 1.4 to 1.8 kg/3 to 4 lb fish bones and heads (white fish only), well rinsed
- 2 onions, sliced
- 1 carrot, sliced
- 1 stalk celery, sliced
- 1 leek, split lengthwise, sliced and well rinsed
- 4 sprigs fresh parsley
- 1 teaspoon salt
- 1 teaspoon black peppercorns
- 2 sprigs fresh thyme (optional)

FISH MIXTURE

- 1.4 kg/3 lb white fish fillets, such as cod, whiting, snapper, (a little carp or pike can be mixed in)
- 2 onions, quartered
- Salt
- 3 eggs, lightly beaten
- ½ teaspoon fresh ground white pepper
- ¼ teaspoon grated nutmeg (optional)
- 60 g/2 oz medium matzo meal
- 1 carrot, thinly sliced
- Fresh parsley sprigs and lemon slices to garnish
- Horseradish-Beetroot Sauce (see page 15), for serving

☐ Prepare stock. Into a large stockpot, place all ingredients for fish stock. Cover with cold water and, over high heat, bring to a boil. Skim off any foam that comes to the surface. Reduce heat and simmer for 20 minutes. Strain stock into a large saucepan or casserole. Set aside.

☐ Prepare fish mixture. Into a food processor fitted with metal blade, place fish and onions and process to a fine purée. (You may need to work in batches.) Add 1½ teaspoons salt, or to taste, eggs, pepper and nutmeg and process to mix.

☐ Stir in matzo meal; add 60 ml/2 fl oz water, a little at a time. The mixture should be light and slightly sticky, but hold its shape. Cover and refrigerate for 30 minutes.

☐ Using 2 tablespoons, form mixture into ovals, placing each on a baking sheet sprinkled with water. Continue until all mixture is shaped.

☐ Bring stock to a boil. Add carrot slices and carefully drop fish ovals into stock. Reduce heat and simmer gently for 1 hour. (Do not leave water to boil.)

☐ Leave fish to cool in stock. Using a slotted spoon, remove fish ovals to a large shallow baking dish or serving platter. Strain stock over the fish ovals and place a carrot slice on top of each oval; scatter remaining slices around the dish. Refrigerate 4 hours or overnight. Garnish with parsley sprigs and lemon slices and serve with Horseradish-Beetroot Sauce.

CURRIED FISH FILLETS

SERVES 6

This dish comes from one of the Jewish communities in India, the southern city of Cochin. Cochin is near the Kerala Coast which produces fresh fish and is also famous for its spice market. This is best served with rice.

- 1 tablespoon vegetable oil
- 1 onion, cut in half and thinly sliced
- 2 to 3 garlic cloves, peeled and finely chopped
- 1 kg/2 lb white fish fillets, such as cod, halibut or whiting, cut in 7.5 cm/3 in pieces
- 45 g/1½ oz fresh coriander leaves, chopped
- 1 tablespoon white- or red-wine vinegar
- 4 tablespoons tomato paste
- 1 teaspoon ground cumin
- ½ teaspoon turmeric
- 1 small fresh red chilli, or ½ teaspoon red-pepper flakes
- Fresh coriander sprigs for garnish
- Hot boiled rice for serving

☐ In a large frying pan, over medium-high heat, heat oil. Add sliced onion and cook until softened and beginning to colour, 3 to 5 minutes. Add garlic and cook 1 minute longer.

☐ Add fish and cook until the fish begins to firm and turn opaque, 4 to 5 minutes. Gently stir in remaining ingredients, except garnish and rice, and 125 ml/4 fl oz water and simmer 15 minutes, covered. The fish will flake easily if tested with the tip of a knife.

☐ Remove fish fillets to a serving dish. Increase heat to high and cook sauce until slightly thickened, 2 to 3 minutes. Pour over fish fillets. Garnish with coriander sprigs and serve with hot rice.

BAKED SALMON WITH AVOCADO-DILL SAUCE

SERVES 12 TO 14

A whole fish baked in foil makes an ideal party or holiday dish. It can be served hot or cold and is kosher for Passover. Poaching a fish requires a large fish kettle or poacher, but baking it gives excellent results as well. If the fish is too big to fit on a baking sheet, cut it in half, then reassemble it for serving. Fish seems tastiest served at room temperature; just as well, as this provides time for adding festive garnishes and preparing sauces and accompaniments.

- 1 2.25 to 2.7 kg/5 to 6 lb whole salmon or sea trout, dressed with head and tail
- Salt
- 1 lemon, sliced
- 4 to 5 spring onions, cut in half lengthwise
- 3 to 4 fresh parsley sprigs
- 3 to 4 fresh dill sprigs
- Vegetable oil
- Thin slices of cucumber (optional)
- Salad leaves, fresh dill sprigs, and lemon slices for garnish

AVOCADO-DILL SAUCE

- 1 large avocado
- 6 sprigs fresh dill
- ½ teaspoon salt
- 4 egg yolks
- Freshly ground black pepper
- 60 ml/2 fl oz lemon juice or cider vinegar, or half and half
- 125 g/4 oz unsalted butter or soft margarine
- Cayenne pepper

☐ Preheat oven to 180°C/350°F/Gas Mark 4. Wash fish, inside and out, under cold running water; do not dry. Sprinkle cavity with salt and stuff with lemon, spring onions, parsley and dill.

☐ Lightly grease a wide piece of foil long enough to enclose fish. Centre foil lengthwise on a large baking sheet and place fish in centre. Bring 2 long ends up over fish and fold together, stopping a few inches from fish; bring together and fold up short sides of foil, forming a large envelope around fish with lots of room for expansion.

☐ Bake fish in foil for 1 hour. Leave fish to cool slightly, about 15 minutes, before unwrapping. Carefully fold back foil, reserve juices if using for a sauce, or discard.

☐ Using a long thin knife, cut along length of backbone. Beginning behind head, peel off skin, pulling out fins as you go, until you reach tail. Scrape off thin layer of brown flesh which runs down the centre of fish.

☐ Carefully centre serving platter over skinned fish and, holding fish on baking sheet against serving platter, flip them over so skinned side of fish is against serving plate. Remove skin and brown flesh from top side. Clean edges of plate.

☐ To serve, arrange salad leaves around fish and garnish fish with thin slices of cucumber, overlapping to imitate scales, or garnish with dill sprigs and lemon slices. Cover loosely and refrigerate until ready to serve. Accompany with Avocado-Dill Sauce.

☐ Make sauce. Cut avocado in half, remove stone and peel off skin. In a food processor fitted with metal blade, process avocado flesh until smooth. Scrape into a mixing bowl and scrape processor clean.

☐ Into processor, place dill, salt and egg yolks and process until dill is finely chopped; season with pepper to taste.

☐ In a small saucepan, over high heat, bring lemon juice or vinegar to a boil. With processor running, slowly pour boiling liquid over yolk mixture and process 1 minute.

☐ In same saucepan, over medium-high heat, bring butter or margarine to a boil. With processor running, slowly pour in hot butter or margarine. Stop processor, add avocado purée and a pinch of cayenne pepper and process 1 minute longer or until well blended and smooth. Taste for seasoning and pour into serving bowl. Refrigerate until ready to serve.

COOK'S TIP

FISH IS BEST SERVED COOL OR AT ROOM TEMPERATURE. IF PREPARING AHEAD, REMOVE FISH FROM REFRIGERATOR 2 TO 3 HOURS BEFORE SERVING.

Jewish-Style Fried Fish

SERVES 6

Introduced by Sephardic Jews in the 1600s, fried fish is now a favourite Friday night supper among many Jewish communities. Somehow it tastes better cold than hot, so it is an ideal choice for a Sabbath supper, as it can be prepared early in the day. Be sure to fry in oil, not butter, and keep in a cool place, not the refrigerator if possible, as the fish will stay crisper much longer. A mixture of half medium and half fine matzo meal is best for the coating.

- 1.4 kg/3 lb fish fillets or steaks, such as halibut, salmon, herring, or any combination
- Salt
- 90 g/3 oz plain flour
- 2 eggs, beaten
- ¼ teaspoon freshly ground black pepper
- 125 g/4 oz matzo meal
- Vegetable oil for frying
- Lemon wedges and parsley sprigs for garnish

☐ Rinse fish fillets or steaks in cold water and sprinkle lightly with salt. Place in a colander and leave to drain for 30 minutes. Pat dry with paper towels.

☐ Into 3 pie plates or shallow dishes, place flour, beaten eggs, seasoned with black pepper, and matzo meal. Dip each piece of fish first into flour, shaking off any excess; then into the egg and brush to coat evenly, finally into matzo meal. Be sure the fish is completely coated with meal to prevent any moisture escaping during frying.

☐ In a deep-fat fryer or large frying pan, over medium-high heat, heat about 1.25 cm/½ in vegetable oil to 180°C/350°F. Add several pieces of fish and fry until underside is well browned, 4 to 5 minutes. Using a fish slice, gently turn fish and fry until other side is brown, 3 to 4 minutes. Remove to paper towels to drain.

☐ Continue frying in batches until all fish is fried, adding more oil as necessary. (Do not try to fry too many pieces at a time or the temperature of the oil will fall too low and the fish will "stew" rather than fry.)

☐ Arrange fish on a serving dish and store in a cool place, loosely covered. Serve with lemon wedges and parsley sprigs. (Fish can be served hot; keep pieces warm in a 180°C/350°F/Gas Mark 4 oven until all fish is cooked, then serve at once.)

Red Snapper with Green Sauce

SERVES 6

When I spent a summer in Mexico with a Jewish-Mexican family many years ago, they baked fish or chicken in a vegetable and herb purée "blanket", which kept the flesh moist and tender. This was made by hand in a mortar and pestle, but the food processor now makes this work easy.

- Vegetable oil for greasing
- 1.4 to 1.8 kg/3 to 4 lb red snapper or sea bass fillets
- Fresh juice of 5 limes
- Salt
- Freshly ground black pepper
- Cherry tomatoes, ripe olives and chopped fresh coriander leaves for garnish

SAUCE

- 1 head Cos lettuce, trimmed, cored and shredded
- ½ cucumber, peeled and seeded
- 1 small green pepper, cored, seeded and chopped
- 1 red onion, quartered
- 3 to 4 garlic cloves
- 1 small bunch watercress, stems trimmed
- 4 to 5 spring onions, trimmed
- 30 g/1 oz coriander leaves

☐ Lightly grease a deep baking dish. Place fish in centre of dish and rub with a little lime juice. Sprinkle with salt and pepper to taste. Set aside.

☐ Make the sauce. In a food processor fitted with metal blade, process lettuce, cucumber, green pepper, red onion, garlic, watercress, spring onions and coriander leaves with remaining lime juice. Pour sauce over fish, cover and refrigerate at least 2 hours.

☐ Preheat oven to 180°C/350°F/Gas Mark 4. Uncover fish and bake, basting twice, until fish is opaque and flesh flakes when pierced with a knife, 20 to 25 minutes. Remove fish to serving platter. Pour sauce over and garnish with cherry tomatoes, ripe olives and coriander leaves.

Baked Trout with Pomegranate

SERVES 4

This dish is typical of the kind of "New Wave" Jewish cooking happening in Israel today. Trout farms have been introduced to the Galilee region, and this classic Western fish has now become very popular. Pomegranates are one of the many exotic fruits widely available in the Middle East and historically important in Jewish cooking.

- 1 large ripe pomegranate
- 1 tablespoon olive oil
- 1 onion, finely chopped
- 2 garlic cloves, peeled and finely chopped
- 125 g/4 oz pecans, coarsely chopped
- 4 tablespoons chopped fresh parsley
- Salt
- Freshly ground black pepper
- ¼ teaspoon ground cardamom
- 2 tablespoons wine vinegar
- 60 g/2 oz butter or margarine, melted
- 4 trout, 300 to 375 g/10 to 12 oz each, cleaned and dressed
- Curly kale for garnish

☐ With a sharp knife, cut top off pomegranate. Score fruit in about 6 wedges and pull apart into separate sections. Gently scoop seeds into a small bowl. Set aside.

☐ In a medium frying pan, over medium-high heat, heat olive oil. Add onion and cook until softened and beginning to colour, 3 to 5 minutes. Add garlic and cook 1 minute longer.

☐ Stir in pecans, parsley, salt and black pepper to taste, cardamom, vinegar and half melted butter or margarine. Remove from heat. Stir in three-quarters of the pomegranate seeds.

☐ Preheat oven to 200°C/400°F/Gas Mark 6. Lightly grease a large shallow baking dish. Rinse fish under cold running water and pat dry with paper towels. Score each fish in 2 places on each side. Spoon one-quarter of the onion mixture into each fish.

☐ Arrange fish in baking dish, drizzle with remaining butter or margarine and bake, uncovered, until flesh flakes easily if tested with tip of a knife, 12 to 15 minutes. Serve fish on a bed of curly kale and sprinkle with pomegranate seeds.

Sweet-and-Sour Fish

SERVES 6

In Eastern Europe, sweet-and-sour fish was generally prepared with carp. In France it is known as *carpe à la Juive* (Jewish-style carp) and it was traditional to serve the head of the fish to the head of the house on the Jewish New Year, Rosh Hashana. This recipe uses fish steaks rather than a whole fish.

- 6 fish steaks, such as carp, pike, salmon or trout, 2.5 cm/1 in thick (1.4 kg/3 lb total weight)
- Salt
- Freshly ground black pepper
- 1 onion, thinly sliced
- 1 carrot, thinly sliced
- 1 bay leaf
- 4 to 6 whole cloves
- 1 lemon, sliced and pips removed
- 2 to 4 slices fresh ginger root
- 1 tablespoon black peppercorns
- 125 ml/4 fl oz red-wine vinegar
- 125 g/4 oz light brown sugar
- 90 g/3 oz raisins
- 4 ginger biscuits, crushed to crumbs (optional)
- 3 to 4 tablespoons chopped fresh parsley
- Lemon twists for garnish

☐ Rinse fish steaks under cold running water and pat dry with paper towels. Sprinkle lightly with salt and pepper to taste and set aside.

☐ In a large, non-aluminium deep frying pan combine onion, carrot, bay leaf, cloves, lemon slices, ginger root and peppercorns with 900 ml/1½ pt cold water. Over high heat, bring to a boil, then simmer, covered, for 15 minutes.

☐ Add fish steaks and cook over medium-low heat, covered, until fish pulls away from centre bone and turns opaque, 10 to 12 minutes. Using a fish slice, carefully remove fish steaks to a large deep glass or ceramic baking dish.

☐ Bring cooking liquid to a boil again and cook until liquid is reduced by half, 7 to 10 minutes. Strain into a smaller saucepan and add the vinegar, brown sugar and raisins. Simmer 2 to 3 minutes longer, stir in the ginger biscuit crumbs, if using, and chopped parsley. Cool slightly, then pour over fish. Cool completely, then refrigerate overnight. Serve chilled, garnished with lemon twists.

ABOVE SUCCULENT FISH PULLED FROM THE BOUNTIFUL WATERS OF THE TURKISH COAST.

Accompaniments

Leek Fritters
Latkes
New Year Carrot Tzimmes Loaf
Sweet-and-Sour Red Cabbage
Spicy Indian-Style Potatoes
Homemade Noodles
Savoury Noodle Kugel
Sweet Potato and Parsnip Kugel
Kreplach
Kasha Varnishkes
Fidellos Tostados
Indian Rice with Tomatoes and Spinach
Romanian-Style Mamaliga
Chelou
Quick-and-Easy Couscous

LEEK FRITTERS

SERVES 4

Leeks are an ancient vegetable, frequently used in the Sephardic Jewish kitchens. These leek patties are eaten at Passover by Greek Jews. They make a delicious vegetable accompaniment to roast poultry and meat dishes. A more hearty version made with minced meat is served as a main course.

- 1 kg/2 lb leeks, split in half lengthwise and well rinsed
- 2 eggs, beaten
- At least 30 g/1 oz fine matzo meal (cake meal)
- Salt
- Freshly ground black pepper
- ½ teaspoon dried thyme
- ¼ teaspoon ground cinnamon
- Vegetable oil for frying
- Lemon wedges for serving

☐ In a large frying pan half filled with water, over high heat, boil leeks until just tender, 5 to 7 minutes. Drain under cold running water.

☐ On a cutting board, chop leeks finely. Squeeze in a clean tea towel to remove any excess liquid. Remove to a large bowl.

☐ Stir in beaten eggs, matzo meal, salt and pepper to taste, thyme and cinnamon until well blended. Batter should be soft enough to drop by spoonfuls; add a little more matzo meal or water if necessary.

☐ In a large, deep frying pan, over medium-high heat, heat about 2.5 cm/1 in oil or enough to just cover fritters. Drop batter by tablespoonful into the hot oil and cook until underside is browned, 2 minutes. Turn and cook until second side is browned, 1 minute longer.

☐ Remove to a serving platter and keep warm in a 150°C/ 300°F/Gas Mark 2 oven. Continue until all batter is used, adding a little more oil if necessary. Serve immediately, garnished with lemon wedges.

LATKES

SERVES 6 TO 8

Latkes are a well-known and well-loved vegetable dish in the Jewish repertoire. Cooked in oil, these potato pancakes are traditional at Hanukah because they symbolize the miracle of the oil which lasted eight days. They are delicious with rich roast poultry, such as duck and goose, but can also be eaten as a brunch dish or on their own sprinkled with sugar or topped with apple sauce or sour cream. Even before the days of the food processor, my mother's were the best.

- 6 medium potatoes, peeled
- 1 onion
- 2 eggs, lightly beaten
- 60 g/2 oz fine matzo meal, or plain flour
- 1 teaspoon salt
- Pinch ground white pepper
- Vegetable oil for frying
- Apple sauce or sour cream for serving

☐ In a food processor fitted with grater attachment, grate potatoes and onion. Drain in a colander, pressing to squeeze out as much liquid as possible. Place in a large bowl and beat in remaining ingredients except oil and accompaniments. (Work as quickly as possible so potatoes do not turn brown.)

☐ In a large, heavy frying pan over medium-high heat, heat about 2.5 cm/1 in vegetable oil or just enough to cover pancakes. Drop batter by tablespoonsful into hot oil and cook until underside is browned, 2 minutes. Turn and cook until second side is browned, 1 to 2 minutes longer.

☐ Remove to a serving platter and keep warm in a 150°C/300°F/Gas Mark 2 oven. Continue until all batter is used, adding a little more oil if necessary. Serve immediately with apple sauce or sour cream.

New Year Carrot Tzimmes Loaf

SERVES 8 TO 10

Carrots symbolize prosperity and hope because of their rich golden colour, so they are served at the New Year, Rosh Hashana. They are often the base of a meatless tzimmes, a composite stew, or bake. In Yiddish, a tzimmes means a mess or a fuss; to make a tzimmes over someone or something means to make a great fuss – usually the grandmothers' province.

This recipe is particularly fussy, but is well worth the effort and can be prepared ahead. Using traditional ingredients, I based this version on an appetizer I used to prepare at the Quai d'Orsay restaurant in Paris, Chef Antoine Bouterin's individual carrot "pâtés" made with carrots and blanched artichokes and served with a butter sauce. This is an ideal recipe for a big holiday dinner.

- 2 leeks, cut in half lengthwise and well rinsed
- 2 large carrots, cooked and mashed
- 1 large sweet potato, cooked and mashed
- 2 tablespoons pareve margarine, melted, or vegetable oil
- 2 tablespoons honey
- 1 tablespoon lemon juice
- Salt
- Freshly ground black pepper
- ¼ teaspoon cayenne pepper, or to taste
- ¼ teaspoon grated nutmeg
- 4 spring onions, finely chopped
- 4 eggs
- 2 egg yolks
- 2 large potatoes, cooked and mashed
- 14 oz/425 g pitted prunes, soaked in hot water 10 to 15 minutes
- Fresh parsley sprigs and lemon twists for garnish

☐ Fill a large saucepan with water and, over high heat, bring to a boil. Add leeks and cook until slightly softened and the colour brightens, 1 to 2 minutes. Drain and rinse under cold running water to stop the cooking and keep colour. Separate and remove to a clean tea towel and drain and dry well. Set aside.

☐ In a large bowl, combine mashed carrots and sweet potato with melted margarine or oil, honey, lemon juice, salt and pepper to taste, cayenne pepper, nutmeg and half the chopped spring onions. Set aside.

☐ In a small bowl, beat 2 of the eggs and 1 yolk. Stir into carrot-sweet potato mixture. Set aside.

☐ In another bowl, place mashed potatoes. Season with salt and pepper and add the remaining spring onions. In another small bowl, beat remaining 2 eggs and 1 yolk. Add to potato-spring onion mixture, beating until well blended.

☐ Preheat oven to 190°C/375°F/Gas Mark 5. Lightly grease a 23.5 × 12.5 × 7.5 cm/9 × 5 × 3 in loaf tin or long terrine dish. Lay leeks across tin or dish, overlapping each slice and alternating tops and bottoms, so tin or dish is lined with white and green parts. Leave leeks to hang over sides of tin or dish.

☐ Drain prunes and pat dry with paper towels. Carefully spoon in half of the carrot-sweet potato mixture, smoothing to make an even bottom layer. Place one-third of the prunes on to carrot layer, leaving space between prunes. Cover with half the potato-spring onion mixture, smoothing top to make an even layer. Sprinkle in another third of the prunes. Repeat layers with the remaining carrot-sweet potato mixture, prunes and potato-spring onion mixture.

☐ Fold over ends of leeks to cover top of tin or dish and cover tightly with foil.

☐ Place tin or dish in a shallow roasting tin or baking dish. Fill the roasting tin with boiling water to about 4 cm/1½ in up side of loaf tin or terrine. Bake 1¼ hours, until knife inserted in centre comes out clean, adding water to water bath if necessary. Cool tzimmes loaf completely in water bath.

☐ Remove loaf tin or dish from water bath and dry bottom of tin. Place on a dish and weight the top overnight.

☐ To serve, unmould and slice into thin slices. Run a sharp knife around edges of tin, shake gently to unmould onto serving plate. Serve chilled, the slices garnished with parsley sprigs and lemon twists.

COOK'S TIP

To weight loaf, cut a thin piece of cardboard the size of top of loaf. Wrap with foil and press against surface of the loaf. Place 2 heavy cans on top of board; refrigerate overnight. To slice loaf, use a sharp thin-bladed knife. Run under hot water and wipe dry before cutting each slice.

SWEET-AND-SOUR RED CABBAGE

SERVES 6 TO 8

Cabbage is an important ingredient in the Jewish kitchen, especially among Russian and Central European Jews, who, unfortunately, mostly overcooked it. This braised cabbage dish is especially delicious with rich meats, such as goose, duck and pot roasts. Made with green cabbage, I serve it with turkey and it is always popular.

- 2 tablespoons vegetable oil
- 1 onion, cut in half and thinly sliced
- 2 dessert apples, peeled, cored and thinly sliced
- 1 red cabbage, about 750 g/ 1½ lb, quartered, cored and shredded
- 60 ml/2 fl oz red-wine vinegar
- 2 to 3 tablespoons light brown sugar
- 60 g/2 oz sultanas (optional)
- 125 ml/4 fl oz vegetable stock or water
- Salt
- Freshly ground black pepper

☐ In a large, heavy-bottomed, non-aluminium pan, over medium-high heat, heat oil. Add onion and cook until soft and golden, 5 to 7 minutes. Add sliced apples and cook until beginning to brown, 2 to 3 minutes.

☐ Add cabbage and remaining ingredients. Simmer, covered, stirring occasionally and adding water if necessary, until cabbage is tender, 30 to 40 minutes. Uncover and cook until liquid is absorbed. Spoon into serving bowl.

COOK'S TIP

SWEET-AND-SOUR CABBAGE IS ALSO DELICIOUS SERVED COLD. IF YOU WANT TO MAKE THE GREEN CABBAGE VERSION, USE WHITE-WINE VINEGAR OR LEMON JUICE AND WHITE SUGAR.

SPICY INDIAN-STYLE POTATOES

SERVES 6 TO 8

This is a typical dish made by the Bene Israel Jews, who live in Bombay. I like the addition of green peas for colour.

- 1.4 kg/3 lb waxy new or red potatoes, unpeeled and chopped
- 5 to 6 tablespoons vegetable oil
- Salt
- ½ teaspoon turmeric
- ½ teaspoon ground cumin
- ½ teaspoon chilli powder
- ½ teaspoon red-pepper flakes, or ¼ teaspoon cayenne pepper
- ½ teaspoon curry powder or garam masala
- 2 teaspoons lemon juice
- 150 g/5 oz green peas (optional)
- Fresh coriander leaves for garnish (optional)

☐ Into a large saucepan, place potatoes. Cover with cold water and, over high heat, bring to a boil. Simmer until just tender, about 20 minutes; do not overcook. Drain potatoes and rinse under cold running water to cool slightly.

☐ Peel potatoes and cut into 2.5 cm/1 in cubes. In a large frying pan, over medium-high heat, heat 4 tablespoons oil. Add salt to taste, turmeric, cumin, chilli powder, red-pepper flakes or cayenne and curry powder or garam masala; stir until well blended.

☐ Add potato cubes and stir to coat with spice mixture, adding a little more oil if necessary. Add lemon juice and 60 ml/2 fl oz water. Cook, covered, 5 minutes.

☐ Uncover and stir in the peas, if using. Cook 2 to 3 minutes longer until peas heat through. Serve garnished with coriander leaves if wished.

Homemade Noodles

SERVES 4 TO 6

Pasta in some form or other is well loved throughout the Jewish world. Lokshen, Yiddish for noodles, are used by Eastern European Jews as an accompaniment to meats, stews, in soups, or in puddings called kugels – egg-enriched dishes of baked noodles with sweet or savoury additions. Italian Jews have pasta as a national dish, Greek and Turkish Jews use macaroni in baked meat dishes and the Middle Eastern and Sephardic Jews use thin noodles or vermicelli called fidellos. This homemade pasta can be cut into soup noodles or any other shape you like. The food processor makes this easy work.

- 250 g/8 oz plain flour
- 2 eggs
- ½ teaspoon salt

☐ In a food processor fitted with metal blade, process flour, eggs and salt until blended. With machine running, add 1 to 2 tablespoons water until dough forms a ball in the machine. (If dough is too sticky, add a little more flour.) Process 30 seconds.

☐ Turn out dough on to a lightly floured surface and knead lightly until dough is smooth and elastic. Cover dough on surface with inverted bowl and leave to rest 30 minutes.

☐ Flour 2 large baking sheets. Cut dough in half and work with one half at a time. On lightly floured surface, roll dough as thin as possible into a 35 cm/14 in square. Place dough square on floured baking sheet and sprinkle with flour; leave to dry 25 to 30 minutes. Repeat with second half of dough.

☐ When dough is slightly dry, fold each square sheet of pasta into a loose, flat Swiss-roll shape. Slice crosswise into noodles 3 mm to 1.25 cm/⅛ to ½ in wide.

☐ Unroll noodles and shake to separate, letting them stand 1 minute longer. (For later use, hang noodles over the back of a chair or wooden rack to dry.)

☐ Bring a large saucepan of water to a boil. Add noodles and cook about 5 minutes for wide noodles and 2 to 3 minutes for thin noodles. Drain and add to boiling chicken soup or toss with butter and cheese and serve immediately.

VARIATIONS

Noodle Squares (Plaetschen)

Prepare dough as above, but do not cut into noodles. Cut the dough squares into 1.25 cm/½ in strips, then cut strips into 1.25 cm/½ in pieces, to form 1.25 cm/½ in squares. Boil as above, use in soup.

Bow Ties (Shpaertzlen)

Roll out dough as directed but do not leave to dry. Cut dough into 2.5 cm/1 in strips, then cut strips into 2.5 cm/1 in pieces to form 2.5 cm/1 in squares. Pinch squares in centre to form bow ties. Boil as above; use in soups and with stews.

Thimble Noodles (Fingerheutchen)

Prepare dough as above, but dry only 15 minutes. Fold dough sheet in half lengthwise and, with a floured thimble or tiny round cutter, cut through the double layer of pasta. Fry pasta circles in oil heated to 190°C/375°F until golden brown and slightly puffed. Drain on paper towels, then serve in chicken soup.

SAVOURY NOODLE KUGEL

A kugel is a baked pudding popular with Eastern European Jews. Traditionally, a kugel was simmered in a separate dish, inside or alongside a cholent (see page 59) and then served as an accompaniment or afterwards with pickles. Noodle kugels can be made with sugar and fresh or dried fruits to be served as a dessert. Cheese-based kugels can be served as an accompaniment dish or a main dish dairy meal for Shavuot.

- 125 g/4 oz unsalted butter or pareve margarine, at room temperature
- 250 g/8 oz cream cheese, at room temperature
- 250 g/8 oz cottage cheese
- 5 eggs, beaten
- 450 ml/¾ pt milk
- Grated zest and juice of 1 lemon
- 2 spring onions, finely chopped
- 45 g/1½ oz raisins (optional)
- Salt
- Freshly ground black pepper
- ¼ teaspoon grated nutmeg
- 250 g/8 oz broad or fine egg noodles, cooked and drained

☐ Preheat oven to 180°C/350°F/Gas Mark 4. Lightly grease a deep baking dish. In a large bowl, cream butter and cream cheese together until smooth and well blended. Beat in cottage cheese and eggs, then slowly beat in the milk.

☐ Stir in lemon zest and juice, spring onions, raisins, if using, salt and pepper to taste and nutmeg. Add noodles and toss to mix well.

☐ Turn into baking dish and cook until mixture is set and top is puffy and golden brown, 1 hour. Serve hot or cold from dish.

VARIATION

BAKE KUGEL IN A WELL-GREASED RING MOULD. COOK 45 TO 50 MINUTES AND UNMOULD ON TO SERVING PLATTER. CUT IN WEDGES TO SERVE.

SWEET POTATO AND PARSNIP KUGEL

SERVES 6 TO 8

The kugel must be one of the greatest contributions of Jewish cooking to the world. It is a baked pudding which can be savoury or sweet, and, depending on the ingredients, eaten as a vegetable or dessert.

Sweet potatoes, carrots and parsnips are all naturally sweet vegetables. They combine to make a baked vegetable pudding which is particularly delicious with roast turkey and duck.

- 2 sweet potatoes, peeled
- 2 carrots, peeled
- 2 parsnips, peeled
- 1 apple, peeled, cored and quartered
- 1 onion, quartered
- 60 g/2 oz butter, margarine or pareve margarine
- Salt
- Freshly ground black pepper
- 1 teaspoon ground cinnamon
- ½ teaspoon grated nutmeg
- 60 g/2 oz light brown sugar
- 4 tablespoons light molasses or golden syrup
- 2 eggs, beaten
- 30 g/1 oz fine matzo meal (cake meal)
- 60 ml/2 fl oz vegetable oil

☐ In a food processor fitted with grater attachment, grate potatoes, carrots, parsnips and apple. Scrape into large bowl and set aside. Wipe processor clean. Grate onion.

☐ Preheat oven to 190°C/375°F/Gas Mark 5. In a large deep frying pan, over medium-high heat, melt butter or margarine. Add onion and cook until beginning to soften, 2 to 3 minutes. Stir in grated vegetables and apple and cook just until vegetables begin to soften, 4 to 5 minutes. Scrape into large bowl.

☐ Add salt and pepper to taste, cinnamon, nutmeg, brown sugar, molasses or golden syrup and 60 ml/2 fl oz water. Stir well and leave to cool slightly. Add beaten eggs and matzo meal.

☐ In a medium roasting tin or 22.5 × 32.5 cm/9 × 13 in baking tin, heat vegetable oil. When a small amount of vegetable mixture sizzles when added to the oil, turn vegetable mixture into the baking tin, smoothing the top evenly. Bake, covered with foil, 30 minutes. Uncover and bake until vegetables feel soft when pierced with a knife and top is brown, 15 to 20 minutes longer.

KREPLACH

MAKES ABOUT 75

Yiddish for "little crêpe", kreplach were originally from Russia and Poland. These are small filled dumplings, sometimes referred to as Jewish ravioli or Jewish wontons. They can be made in various shapes and filled with meat, chicken, or cheese when used at Shavuot. The meat filling is usually made from the shin of beef which has been used to make the stock for the soup on Purim or before the Yom Kippur fast, but minced beef can be used instead.

- 250 g/8 oz cooked beef, minced, or 250 g/8 oz minced beef, browned
- 1 small onion, chopped
- ½ teaspoon salt
- Freshly ground black pepper
- 1 tablespoon chopped fresh dill (optional)
- 1 egg
- 1 recipe Homemade Noodles dough (see page 78)

COOK'S TIP

KREPLACH CAN BE SERVED OTHER WAYS. COOK IN BOILING WATER AS DIRECTED AND SERVE TOSSED WITH OIL AND PARSLEY OR TOMATO SAUCE. FOR A MAIN DAIRY MEAL, FRY CHEESE-FILLED KREPLACH IN OIL AND A LITTLE CHOPPED ONION AND SPRINKLE WITH CHEESE.

☐ Into a food processor fitted with metal blade, process beef and chopped onion until finely chopped but not pasty. Add salt and pepper to taste, dill, if using, and the egg and, with pulse action, process until meat mixture is moist and holds together. Scrape into a bowl and refrigerate until ready to use.

☐ Prepare noodle dough and roll out as directed but do not leave to dry. Cut into 5 cm/2 in squares. Put 1 teaspoon filling in the centre of each square and brush corners with a little water. Fold lower-left corner over upper-right corner to form a triangle, pressing the edges firmly together to seal.

☐ Transfer to a lightly floured baking sheet and continue until all dough is used. (Kreplach can be made up to this point ahead and refrigerated until ready to cook.)

☐ Bring a large saucepan of water to a boil. Add some of the kreplach but do not overcrowd. Simmer gently 12 to 15 minutes. With a slotted spoon, remove and drain in a colander. Bring water back to a boil and continue until all kreplach are tender. (Cooked kreplach can be refrigerated or frozen for future use.)

☐ To serve, simmer kreplach in chicken or meat soup until heated through, 10 to 12 minutes. Serve piping hot.

CHEESE FILLING

COMBINE 500 G/1 LB COTTAGE CHEESE, 2 TABLESPOONS SOUR CREAM, 3 TABLESPOONS FINE BREADCRUMBS OR MATZO MEAL, SALT AND PEPPER TO TASTE, 1 TABLESPOON CHOPPED FRESH PARSLEY, 1 TABLESPOON SNIPPED FRESH CHIVES AND 1 EGG. MIX WELL AND REFRIGERATE UNTIL READY TO SERVE.

KASHA VARNISHKES

SERVES 6 TO 8

Kasha, or roasted buckwheat, is a staple grain of poor Russian Jews because it is hearty and nourishing. There are two versions of this dish. The one eaten on Purim is a simple dish of sautéed onions with kasha and pasta bow ties. The original version, however, is like a little turnover, or varnishke, filled with kasha and mushrooms.

- 175 g/6 oz kasha
- 1 egg, lightly beaten
- ½ teaspoon salt
- Freshly ground black pepper
- 450 ml/¾ pt vegetable stock or water
- 1 tablespoon vegetable oil
- 500 g/1 lb mushrooms, coarsely chopped
- 1 recipe Homemade Noodles dough (see page 78)
- Oil for frying

☐ In a bowl combine kasha and beaten egg until kasha grains are well coated. Place kasha-egg mixture in a heavy-bottomed frying pan and cook over medium heat until all grains are separate, 3 to 5 minutes.

☐ Sprinkle in salt and pepper to taste. Stir in vegetable stock or water and cook, covered, over medium-low heat, for 10 minutes, adding a little more liquid if necessary.

☐ In a medium frying pan, over medium-high heat, heat oil. Add mushrooms and cook until tender and most liquid is evaporated, 5 to 7 minutes.

☐ Uncover kasha and stir. Add cooked mushrooms and cook on medium-low heat until all liquid is absorbed, 3 to 5 minutes. Cool completely.

☐ Prepare noodle dough as directed but roll out into a large rectangle 3 mm/⅛ in thick. Using a 7.5 cm/3 in round cutter, cut as many dough circles as possible; reroll trimmings.

☐ Place 1 teaspoon kasha filling on to centre of each dough circle. Brush the edge of dough with a little water and fold dough circle in half. Using a fork, press edges together to seal.

☐ Bring a large saucepan of water to a boil. Add the varnishkes and cook until tender, 12 to 15 minutes. Drain carefully in a colander. Serve in soup, with gravy, or fry in oil and serve hot.

ABOVE THE DATE HARVEST AT A KIBBUTZ IN THE BETH SHEAN VALLEY, ISRAEL.

EASY KASHA VARNISHKES

PREPARE KASHA AS ABOVE (WITH OR WITHOUT MUSHROOMS). FRY 1 FINELY CHOPPED ONION IN 2 TABLESPOONS OIL UNTIL SOFT AND GOLDEN, 3 TO 5 MINUTES. STIR IN COOKED KASHA AND 125 G/ 4 OZ COOKED PASTA BOW TIES. TASTE FOR SALT AND PEPPER AND SERVE HOT, OR AS AN ACCOMPANIMENT TO MEAT DISHES.

Fidellos Tostados

SERVES 6

Spanish Sephardic Jews have been eating a very thin vermicelli-like pasta called fidellos for centuries. It is also popular in Greece, introduced by Spanish Jews when they fled Spain during the Inquisition. I have often eaten this dish cooked by a Greek friend of mine, although he sometimes breaks the pasta coils and throws in rice as in this recipe.

- 375 g/12 oz package vermicelli or angel hair pasta in coils
- 100 g/3½ oz American long-grain rice
- 60 ml/2 fl oz olive oil
- 1 215 g/7 oz can tomatoes, drained
- 450 to 750 ml/¾ to 1¼ pt chicken stock or water
- 1 teaspoon salt
- ½ teaspoon dried oregano
- Freshly ground black pepper
- Fresh coriander leaves for garnish

☐ In a dry large, heavy-bottomed frying pan, over medium-high heat, heat pasta and rice until golden brown, stirring frequently, 5 to 7 minutes. (It does not matter if pasta breaks a little.)

☐ Add olive oil, tomatoes, chicken stock or water, salt, oregano and black pepper to taste. Bring to a boil; reduce heat to medium and simmer, stirring often to unwind pasta, 7 to 10 minutes. Reduce heat to low, cover and cook 10 minutes longer until all the liquid is absorbed and pasta and rice are tender. Turn into a serving bowl and garnish with coriander leaves.

INDIAN RICE WITH TOMATOES AND SPINACH

SERVES 6

This is a mild, yet aromatic, rice dish from the Bene Israel Jewish community, near Bombay. Use fresh young spinach leaves if possible. Dhana jeera powder is a mixture of roasted and ground coriander and cumin seeds, available at Indian shops.

- 3 tablespoons vegetable oil
- 1 onion, cut in half and thinly sliced
- 425 g/14 oz basmati or American long-grain rice, rinsed and soaked in cold water for 30 minutes
- 300 g/10 oz young spinach leaves, cooked and squeezed dry, or 1 300 g/10 oz package frozen spinach, thawed and squeezed dry
- 2 medium tomatoes, peeled, seeded and diced
- ¼ teaspoon turmeric
- 1 teaspoon dhana jeera powder (see above), or ¾ teaspoon ground coriander and ¼ teaspoon ground cumin
- Salt
- Freshly ground black pepper

☐ In a large heavy saucepan, over medium-high heat, heat oil. Add onion and cook until softened and golden, 5 to 7 minutes. Drain rice well and add to onion. Cook, stirring constantly, until rice turns translucent and begins to colour, 1 to 2 minutes.

☐ Add spinach, tomatoes, turmeric and dhana jeera powder or coriander and cumin. Add salt and pepper to taste.

☐ Pour in 450 ml/¾ pint water and stir. Bring rice mixture to a boil, then cover tightly and reduce heat to very low. Cook until water is completely absorbed and rice is tender, 25 minutes.

☐ Remove lid and fluff rice gently with a fork, being careful not to disturb the bottom layer which will have formed a crust. Cover and cook 10 minutes longer. Spoon rice into a serving bowl; scrape up browned crisp crust from bottom and spoon around the rice. Serve hot.

ROMANIAN-STYLE MAMALIGA

SERVES 6 TO 8

This classic cornmeal recipe is typical of Romanian-Jewish cooking and is similar to the northern Italian dish of polenta. Without the cheese it makes an ideal accompaniment to braised meats with gravy, such as Old-fashioned Pot Roast with Onion Gravy (see page 58); the addition of cottage cheese makes it an ideal main dairy meal. Originally this was made with Brunza Alba, a Romanian cheese, but curd cheese or cottage cheese make adequate substitutes.

- 300 g/10 oz yellow cornmeal or polenta
- 1 teaspoon salt
- 4 tablespoons oil (optional)
- 500 g/1 lb curd cheese or cottage cheese, drained and sieved

☐ In a medium bowl, mix cornmeal or polenta with 250 ml/8 fl oz cold water until smooth. Bring a large pot filled with 900 ml/1½ pt water to a boil. Add salt, then gradually pour in the moistened cornmeal, stirring constantly to prevent lumps.

☐ Over medium-low heat, cook, stirring constantly with a wooden spoon, until soft and all the water is absorbed, 20 to 35 minutes. Remove from heat and stir in oil, if using, and the curd cheese or cottage cheese. Spoon into a serving bowl and serve immediately.

VARIATION

COOK CORNMEAL AS DIRECTED WITH 750 TO 900 ML/1¼ TO 1½ PT WATER AND STIR IN ONLY 2 TABLESPOONS OIL. SPREAD EVENLY ON TO A LARGE BAKING SHEET OR SWISS-ROLL TIN AND LEAVE TO COOL. WHEN FIRM, TURN OUT ON TO WORK SURFACE AND CUT INTO SQUARES. FRY IN OIL; OR BRUSH WITH OIL AND GRILL UNDER PREHEATED GRILL UNTIL HOT AND BROWNED, 3 TO 5 MINUTES. SERVE WITH ROAST MEATS AND POULTRY OR VEGETABLE STEWS.

ABOVE Indian Rice with Tomatoes and Spinach.

CHELOU

SERVES 6 TO 8

Chelou is a simple dish of steamed rice oven-baked or cooked on top of the stove in a way which forms a crust on the bottom and light fluffy rice above. This is an Iranian dish enjoyed by Jews and non-Jews alike and is traditional at Rosh Hashana. Many other dishes use chelou as the base to which meat, vegetables or a stew of dried herbs and a little meat are added. Sometimes the baking dish or tin is lined with a thin layer of potatoes.

- 1 teaspoon salt
- 425 g/14 oz basmati or other long-grain rice, rinsed and soaked in cold water for 30 minutes
- 4 tablespoons oil, or 2 tablespoons oil and 2 tablespoons butter

☐ In a large, heavy-bottomed saucepan, over high heat, bring at least 2 l/3¼ pt of water and salt to a boil. Drain rice in a sieve under cold running water until water runs clear. Add rice to boiling water and cook until a grain of rice feels almost tender, but is uncooked at centre, 7 to 10 minutes. Stir occasionally, being careful not to bruise rice. Drain rice into a sieve and rinse under warm running water to remove any starch. Drain well.

☐ In another large, heavy-bottomed saucepan or deep frying pan with tight-fitting lid, over medium-high heat, heat 2 tablespoons oil with 60 ml/2 fl oz water until steaming. Spoon rice into the pan, shaking to distribute it evenly. Cover rice with a clean dry tea towel or double layer of paper towels. Cover pan tightly and reduce heat to very low. Cook 15 minutes, remove lid and cloth and, with the handle of a wooden spoon, poke several holes in the rice layer to allow steam to escape.

☐ Sprinkle over remaining 2 tablespoons oil mixed with 2 tablespoons water (see variation for method for butter), cover with cloth or paper towels, and cover tightly and cook 10 to 15 minutes longer.

☐ Uncover pan and remove tea towel or paper towels. Fluff rice gently with a fork, leaving bottom layer intact. Spoon rice into a serving bowl, then scrape the crusty layer from the bottom of the pan and spoon around the fluffy rice. Traditionally, honoured guests got the crispy bits!

VARIATION

IF USING BUTTER FOR A DAIRY MEAL, MELT BUTTER IN 2 TABLESPOONS WATER AND PROCEED AS ABOVE. IF YOU WISH TO ADD POTATO LAYER, COOK RICE AS DIRECTED AND HEAT OIL (OR BUTTER) WITH WATER. COVER BOTTOM OF PAN WITH 2 MEDIUM POTATOES, PEELED AND CUT INTO 5 MM/¼ IN SLICES. COVER POTATOES WITH RICE AND PROCEED AS ABOVE. IN THIS VERSION IT IS POTATOES AND A LITTLE RICE WHICH FORM BOTTOM CRUST.

QUICK-AND-EASY COUSCOUS

SERVES 4

Couscous, a fine semolina made from wheat, is a staple food of North African Jews. It is eaten like rice in the Middle East or pasta in Italy. Once painstakingly slow to prepare, it is now very quick and easy thanks to the quick-cooking variety. It also makes a delightful change. Delicious on its own, it is also the perfect accompaniment for a lamb, beef or vegetable ragout. In North Africa, the couscous is generally steamed in a special piece of equipment called a *couscousier*. It is placed over the simmering stew to cook and then served with the meat or vegetables.

- 250 g/8 oz quick-cooking couscous
- 2 tablespoons olive oil
- 1 small onion, finely chopped
- 2 garlic cloves, finely chopped
- Salt
- Freshly ground black pepper
- 1 teaspoon red-pepper sauce, or ½ teaspoon cayenne pepper
- 1 teaspoon paprika
- 2 tablespoons chopped fresh parsley, coriander or mint

☐ Cook couscous according to manufacturer's directions. Set aside.

☐ In a medium frying pan, over medium-high heat, heat oil. Add onion and cook until onion is soft and beginning to colour, 3 to 5 minutes. Add garlic and cook 1 minute longer. Add salt and pepper to taste, red-pepper sauce or cayenne, paprika and chopped parsley, coriander or mint. Remove from heat and stir into cooked couscous. Serve hot or warm.

Salads

Israeli Salad
Beetroot and Watercress Salad with Mustard Vinaigrette
German-Style Potato Salad
Moroccan Carrot Salad
Cucumber Salad with Dill
Tabbouleh
Avocado and Pomegranate Salad

ISRAELI SALAD

SERVES 4

This simple salad of diced fresh vegetables and olive oil is eaten everywhere in Israel, as an accompaniment to grilled chicken and meats, in pita pockets, and is even eaten for breakfast in some homes. You can add any vegetables you like, but tomato and cucumber are the essentials. The vegetables should be cut into very small dice, about 6 mm/¼ in pieces.

☐ In a large salad bowl, combine cubed tomato, diced cucumber, green pepper, onion and parsley; toss together.

☐ Sprinkle with olive oil, lemon juice and salt and pepper to taste; toss again. Garnish with fresh mint.

- 2 large ripe tomatoes, diced into 6 mm/¼ in cubes
- 1 large, or 2 small, cucumbers, peeled and diced
- 1 green pepper, cored, seeded and diced
- 1 onion, chopped
- 4 tablespoons chopped fresh parsley
- 2 to 3 tablespoons olive oil
- Juice of 1 lemon
- Salt
- Freshly ground black pepper
- Fresh mint leaves for garnish

VARIATION

PREPARE VEGETABLES AS ABOVE BUT DRESS WITH 3 TO 4 TABLESPOONS TAHINI, DILUTED WITH 2 TABLESPOONS LEMON JUICE AND SEASONED WITH SALT AND PEPPER. THIN TO THE DESIRED CONSISTENCY WITH A LITTLE WATER OR MORE LEMON JUICE.

Beetroot and Watercress Salad with Mustard Vinaigrette

SERVES 6

Beetroot has always been a staple in the Russian-Jewish repertoire. It is also served in the Sephardic community with a simple dressing of lemon juice, olive oil and a little chopped fresh parsley or coriander. Here, fresh beetroot is combined with watercress and a classic mustard-based oil and vinegar dressing.

MUSTARD VINAIGRETTE

- 4 tablespoons white-wine vinegar
- Salt
- Freshly ground black pepper
- 1 teaspoon sugar (optional)
- 2 teaspoons Dijon-style mustard
- 150 ml/¼ pt olive oil or vegetable oil, or a combination

- 1 large bunch watercress, or 250 g/8 oz fresh young spinach leaves, trimmed and washed
- 10 to 12 small beetroot, cooked, peeled and thinly sliced or diced
- Fresh coriander leaves for garnish

☐ Prepare vinaigrette. Into a small bowl, place wine vinegar. Add salt and pepper to taste and sugar, if using. Stir in mustard until well blended. With a wire whisk, slowly beat in oil or oils until vinaigrette is smooth and creamy. Set aside.

☐ Arrange watercress or spinach leaves on 6 individual plates. Evenly distribute sliced or diced beetroot among 6 plates. Stir vinaigrette and spoon some over each salad. Garnish with coriander leaves and serve immediately.

German-Style Potato Salad

SERVES 4 TO 6

Although potatoes were not brought to Europe from South America until the 16th century, Jewish communities all over the world took to them in a short period of time. German Jews use potatoes extensively in breads, soups, and dumplings. They also enjoy them in kugels, latkes, and knishes, as well as boiled, fried, and roasted and in hot or cold potato salads. This is my mother's hot potato salad, a non-mayonnaise version.

- 1 kg/2 lb waxy potatoes, cooked, peeled and cut into 1.25 cm/½ in cubes
- 2 German-style dill pickles, diced
- 2 tablespoons vegetable oil
- 1 onion, finely chopped
- 1 garlic clove, finely chopped
- 1 stalk celery, strings removed, finely chopped
- Salt
- Freshly ground black pepper
- 1 tablespoon light brown sugar
- 1 tablespoon German mustard
- 60 ml/2 fl oz red- or white-wine vinegar
- Chopped fresh parsley for garnish

☐ In a large bowl, place warm potatoes. Add diced dill pickles. Set aside.

☐ In a medium frying pan, over medium-high heat, heat oil. Add onion, garlic and celery and cook until onion just begins to soften, 2 to 3 minutes. Add salt and pepper to taste. Stir in sugar, mustard and vinegar until well blended.

☐ Pour over potato-pickle mixture; toss gently to mix. Spoon into serving bowl and sprinkle with parsley for garnish. (If you like, drizzle with additional oil.)

Moroccan Carrot Salad

SERVES 4 TO 6

This is a favourite Middle Eastern salad, popular in Israel. It is sweet and spicy, as well as being colourful. Raw grated carrots can be used, but traditionally the carrots are cooked first.

- 500 g/1 lb carrots, peeled and cooked until just tender, cooking liquid reserved
- 2 tablespoons vegetable oil
- 2 garlic cloves, peeled and finely chopped
- 1 teaspoon salt
- 1½ teaspoons cumin
- ½ teaspoon red-pepper flakes, cayenne pepper or red-pepper sauce
- 1 teaspoon sugar
- 2 to 3 tablespoons chopped fresh parsley
- 3 to 4 tablespoons lemon juice
- Fresh parsley sprigs for garnish

☐ In a food processor fitted with grater blade, or with a box grater, grate carrots into a large bowl. Set aside.

☐ In a medium frying pan, over medium-low heat, heat oil. Add chopped garlic and cook until garlic begins to soften and colour, 2 to 3 minutes. Add salt, cumin, red-pepper flakes, cayenne or red-pepper sauce and sugar, stirring to blend.

☐ Stir in chopped parsley and lemon juice. Slowly pour in 125 to 175 ml/4 to 6 fl oz of the carrot cooking liquid. Bring to a boil and simmer 3 to 5 minutes. Pour over carrots. Cool to room temperature.

☐ Cover and refrigerate 6 to 8 hours or overnight. Spoon into a serving bowl and garnish with parsley sprigs.

Cucumber Salad with Dill

SERVES 4 TO 6

Cucumber salads are popular in most Jewish communities. In Eastern Europe, the preference is for a vinegar-based (or acetic-acid) marinade; in the Middle East, a yogurt base is used for tarator or cacik, traditional cucumber salads. It makes a delicious accompaniment to fish, poultry and lamb dishes and ideal on a buffet table.

- 60 ml/2 fl oz white wine or white distilled vinegar
- 1 to 2 tablespoons sugar
- Salt
- Freshly ground black pepper
- 2 to 3 tablespoons finely chopped fresh dill
- 1 cucumber, lightly peeled

☐ Into a measuring jug, pour vinegar and 125 ml/4 fl oz water. Stir in sugar, salt and pepper to taste. Add chopped dill and stir; set aside.

☐ Using a fork, score the cucumber lengthwise. In a food processor fitted with a slicing disc, thinly slice cucumber. Place in a large bowl and pour marinade over. Refrigerate overnight. Serve chilled.

VARIATION

Omit vinegar marinade. To 250 ml/8 fl oz plain yogurt, add 1 crushed garlic clove, salt and pepper to taste, 1 to 2 tablespoons lemon juice and 1 tablespoon chopped fresh dill or mint. Pour over sliced cucumbers and refrigerate overnight. Serve chilled.

Tabbouleh

SERVES 10 TO 12

This Middle-Eastern cracked wheat salad is an ideal dish for a buffet party and makes a change from a rice salad. The cracked wheat has an earthy flavour, enhanced by the abundant quantity of parsley – it is sometimes referred to as parsley salad. I first tasted this dish at a party in Paris given by an Israeli, and I have been serving it at parties ever since.

- 175 g/6 oz bulgur wheat
- 2 large ripe tomatoes, peeled, seeded and chopped, or 4 to 5 Italian plum tomatoes, finely chopped
- 1 small cucumber, peeled, seeded and finely chopped
- 4 spring onions, finely sliced
- 4 to 6 tablespoons chopped fresh parsley
- 4 to 6 tablespoons chopped fresh mint
- Juice of 2 to 3 lemons
- 175 ml/6 fl oz olive oil
- Salt
- Freshly ground black pepper
- Vine leaves or shredded lettuce
- Cherry tomatoes, sliced olives and mint leaves for garnish

☐ In a large bowl, place bulgur wheat. Cover with cold water and leave to soak overnight or until tender.

☐ Drain in a colander or sieve. Turn on to a clean tea towel and roll in the towel to squeeze dry. Transfer to a large bowl and fluff with a fork.

☐ Add chopped tomatoes, cucumber, sliced spring onions, chopped parsley and chopped mint; toss well to combine. Pour in lemon juice and olive oil and season to taste with salt and pepper. The flavour should be sharp and herby. Refrigerate until ready to serve.

☐ To serve, line a shallow bowl with prepared vine leaves or shredded lettuce. Pile bulgur wheat salad on to lettuce in a pyramid shape and surround with cherry tomatoes, sliced olives and mint leaves.

Avocado and Pomegranate Salad

SERVES 4

Avocados are Israel's top export, and are so popular and plentiful that they are used in many salads and appetizer dishes. Oranges, also a big export fruit, and pomegranates combine perfectly in this salad, which makes an unusual first course or side dish for a meat or dairy dinner.

DRESSING

- 4 tablespoons white-wine vinegar
- 2 tablespoons orange juice
- Salt
- Freshly ground black pepper
- 1 teaspoon honey
- 2 tablespoons olive oil
- 1 tablespoon peanut or sunflower oil
- 2 tablespoons chopped fresh mint

- 1 ripe pomegranate, cut in half
- 175 g/6 oz black grapes, cut in half and pips removed
- 2 ripe avocados
- 1 tablespoon lemon juice
- Fresh mint leaves to garnish

☐ In a small bowl, whisk together wine vinegar, orange juice, salt and pepper to taste and honey. Slowly whisk in olive oil and vegetable oil until dressing is thick and creamy. Stir in the chopped mint. Set aside.

☐ Into a medium bowl, scrape seeds out of pomegranate halves. Add grape halves and toss to mix.

☐ Cut avocados in half and remove stones. Using a round-bladed knife, run it between skin and flesh of avocados, working skin away from flesh until skin is removed.

☐ Place avocados, round-side up, on work surface and, using a sharp knife and starting 1.25 cm/½ in below stalk end, cut avocado lengthwise into 6 mm/¼ in slices, leaving stalk end intact. Arrange each sliced avocado half on 4 individual plates. Using palm of hand, gently push avocado slices forward to fan out slices. Sprinkle lemon juice over them.

☐ Sprinkle one-quarter of the pomegranate seed-grape mixture on to each avocado half and spoon over dressing. Garnish each plate with a few mint leaves.

ABOVE Avocado and Pomegranate Salad.

Desserts

Summer Fruit Compote

Oven-Baked Quinces

Dried Fruit Compote

Israeli Orange Sorbet

Fruit-Filled Lokshen Pudding

Favourite Matzo Pudding

Sliced Exotic Fruits with Dates

Summer Fruit Compote

SERVES 8 TO 10

This is one of the easiest and most versatile summer desserts I know. It can be made with any combination of soft fruit and berries, but I try to use peaches, nectarines and apricots as a base. As the summer progresses, the choice of soft fruits and berries increases and, of course, cherries and grapes are wonderful additions. I always try to freeze some, as the sight of "fruit compote" thrills my husband on a cold winter's night. Following a dairy meal it can be served with whipped cream, yogurt or vanilla ice cream. This is my mother-in-law's recipe.

- 6 ripe peaches, peeled and sliced
- 6 ripe nectarines or plums, sliced
- 6 ripe apricots, sliced
- 1 cinnamon stick (optional)
- Juice of 1 lemon
- 250 g/8 oz ripe black or sweet cherries
- 1 kg/2 lb mixed berries, such as strawberries, cut in half if large, raspberries, blueberries, blackberries, loganberries or redcurrants
- Sugar or artificial sweetener
- Fresh mint leaves for garnish

☐ In a large non-aluminium saucepan, place sliced peaches, nectarines or plums and apricots. Add enough water to barely cover fruit, cinnamon stick (if using) and lemon juice. Over high heat, bring to a boil. Cover and cook over low heat 2 to 3 minutes; do not boil hard or fruit may break apart.

☐ Add cherries and cook, covered, until hard fruits are just tender and the cherries have begun to lose their colour, 2 minutes longer. Add strawberries and cook 1 minute. Add remaining berries and cook, stirring occasionally, until hard fruits are tender and berries just beginning to soften, 2 to 3 minutes. Remove from heat and leave to stand, covered, for 30 minutes.

☐ Stir in sugar or artificial sweetener to taste. Transfer fruit to large serving bowl and refrigerate 3 to 4 hours or overnight. Garnish with fresh mint leaves.

Oven-Baked Quinces

SERVES 8

Quinces are popular with North African and Middle Eastern Jews and, although they require lengthy cooking to tenderize them, they have a texture and perfume which is exotic and tempting.

- 250 ml/8 fl oz lemon juice
- 4 quinces, trimmed, cut in half and cored if you like, but not peeled
- 500 g/1 lb sugar
- 1 cinnamon stick
- Rosewater for sprinkling
- Yogurt for serving (optional)

☐ In a shallow baking dish, place lemon juice. Place quince halves in dish, turning them to cover all sides with lemon juice to prevent them darkening.

☐ In a large, non-aluminium saucepan, place 375 g/12 oz sugar and cinnamon stick. Stir in 450 ml/¾ pt water. Over high heat, bring to a boil, stirring to dissolve sugar.

☐ Gently add quinces and lemon juice and cook, covered, over low heat, until quinces are fork-tender, 20 to 25 minutes. Preheat oven to 230°C/450°F/Gas Mark 8.

☐ Transfer quince halves, cut side up, to a medium baking dish; pour syrup over. Sprinkle quince halves with remaining sugar and bake, uncovered, until sugar caramelizes and the fruit is nicely browned and very tender, 7 to 10 minutes.

☐ Remove from oven and cool to room temperature. Sprinkle with a little rosewater and serve with yogurt if you like.

Dried Fruit Compote

SERVES 10 TO 12

Fruit compotes made from dried fruit are popular with Jews from all over Europe. Throughout long winters, dried fruits were available and made a delicious dessert which could follow a milk or meat meal. Any combination of fruits can be used and the poaching liquid can range from water to tea, fruit juice or wine. After a dairy meal, serve with yogurt or sour cream to cut the natural sweetness.

My family finds the fruit yields enough sweetness, but you can add sugar or honey to taste. Use any combination of dried fruit you like, the bulk being prunes and apricots.

- 215 g/7 oz large pitted prunes
- 215 g/7 oz dried no-soak apricots
- 215 g/7 oz dried no-soak pears
- 100 g/3½ oz dried no-soak peaches
- 100 g/3½ oz dried no-soak apple rings
- 90 g/3 oz raisins
- 4 tablespoons honey or sugar (optional)
- Grated zest and juice of 1 lemon
- Grated zest and juice of 1 orange
- 4 to 6 whole cloves
- 1 cinnamon stick
- 1 tablespoon black peppercorns (optional)
- Slivered blanched almonds, toasted, for garnish

COOK'S TIP

If you like a thicker syrup, remove fruit to a serving bowl. Return liquid to the heat, bring to a boil and reduce 4 to 5 minutes. Strain over fruit and chill as above. Syrup will thicken as it chills.

☐ Into a large non-aluminium saucepan, place prunes, apricots, pears, peaches, apple rings and raisins. Cover with 2 l/3¼ pt water or enough to generously cover fruit.

☐ Stir in honey or sugar to taste, if using, and add grated lemon and orange zests and juices, cloves, cinnamon stick and peppercorns, if using. Over high heat, bring to a boil. Cook, covered, over low heat, until fruit is plump and tender, 20 minutes.

☐ With slotted spoon, remove cloves, cinnamon stick and peppercorns. Spoon fruit into a serving bowl and pour liquid over. Chill 3 to 4 hours or overnight. Sprinkle with toasted almonds for garnish.

Israeli Orange Sorbet

SERVES 6

Citrus fruits are one of Israel's top exports and are available year round. Sorbets and ices are especially popular in the hot climate of the Middle East, as well as the rest of the world. Sorbet makes an ideal dessert choice after any meal – meat or milk – especially if you spoon a little Sabra, an Israeli chocolate-orange liqueur, over each serving.

- 250 g/8 oz sugar
- Grated zest and juice of 1 lemon
- Grated zest of 3 oranges
- 450 ml/¾ pt fresh-squeezed orange juice, strained
- 2 egg whites, beaten to soft peaks
- Fresh mint leaves for garnish
- Sabra (or other orange-flavour liqueur) for serving

☐ In a small heavy saucepan, combine sugar, lemon and orange zests and 250 ml/8 fl oz water. Slowly bring to a boil, stirring until sugar dissolves. Cook 5 minutes; remove from heat and cool and refrigerate 3 to 4 hours or overnight.

☐ Combine lemon and orange juices with the chilled syrup and, if you like, strain for a very smooth sorbet.

☐ If using an ice-cream machine, freeze according to manufacturer's directions.

☐ Alternatively, put into a metal bowl and freeze 3 to 4 hours until semifrozen. Into a food processor fitted with metal blade, scrape the semifrozen mixture; process until light and creamy, 30 to 45 seconds. Return to metal bowl and freeze another 1½ hours. Scrape into food processor again and process with beaten egg whites until well mixed and light and creamy, 30 seconds. Freeze 3 to 4 hours until completely firm.

☐ Soften 5 minutes at room temperature before scooping into individual serving glasses. Garnish with a few mint leaves and pass liqueur, allowing each guest to pour a little over sorbet.

COOK'S TIP

ADDING BEATEN EGG WHITES GIVES SORBET A VERY SMOOTH, CREAMY TEXTURE. IF YOU PREFER A ROUGHER, "ICIER" TEXTURE, OMIT EGG WHITES. PROCESSING MIXTURE BREAKS UP THE ICE CRYSTALS AND CONTRIBUTES TO A SMOOTH TEXTURE.

FRUIT-FILLED LOKSHEN PUDDING

SERVES 4

A sweet kugel is an old-fashioned Ashkenazic dessert – rich and heavy. This creamy version with dried fruits makes a delicious change. Use vermicelli or angel hair pasta for a very creamy pudding.

☐ In a medium saucepan, over medium-high heat, bring milk to a boil. Add noodles and cook over low heat until noodles are just tender and have absorbed most of the milk, 15 minutes. Cool slightly.

☐ Preheat oven to 180°C/350°F/Gas Mark 4. Lightly grease a 900 ml/1½ pt baking dish or soufflé dish. In a large bowl, beat eggs, salt, lemon and orange zests, cinnamon, nutmeg and sugar until well blended. Add melted butter or margarine and dried fruits.

☐ Add cooked pasta to the egg mixture; toss together to distribute the dried fruit evenly. Turn into the baking dish and sprinkle with almonds. Bake until a knife inserted in to the centre comes out clean, 40 to 50 minutes.

- 450 ml/¾ pt milk
- 125 g/4 oz vermicelli, angel hair pasta or thin spaghetti
- 2 eggs
- ¼ teaspoon salt
- Grated zest of 1 lemon
- Grated zest of 1 orange
- ½ teaspoon ground cinnamon
- ¼ teaspoon grated nutmeg
- 60 g/2 oz sugar
- 30 g/1 oz butter or margarine, melted
- 100 g/3½ oz no-soak dried apricots, chopped
- 45 g/1½ oz pitted dates, chopped
- 45 g/1½ oz sultanas
- 30 g/1 oz slivered almonds

COOK'S TIP

FOR A SOFTER, CREAMIER PUDDING, BAKE PUDDING IN A WATER BATH. PREPARE AS ABOVE BUT PLACE BAKING DISH OR SOUFFLÉ DISH INTO A LARGER ROASTING TIN. FILL TIN WITH BOILING WATER TO COME ABOUT HALF WAY UP SIDE OF BAKING DISH. COVER FOR FIRST 25 MINUTES, THEN UNCOVER TO BROWN TOP AND ALMONDS.

FAVOURITE MATZO PUDDING

SERVES 6

Made in the style of a noodle pudding, this pudding replaces the noodles with matzo, making it kosher for Passover. Mix in as many favourite ingredients and spices as you like: the expression "it's a real matzo pudding" means a real mix up or muddle! All ingredients should be kosher for Passover.

- 4 matzos, broken into small pieces
- 1 dessert apple or pear, peeled, cored and grated
- 90 g/3 oz raisins
- 45 g/1½ oz no-soak dried apricots, chopped
- 60 g/2 oz almonds or walnuts, chopped and toasted
- 75 g/2½ oz sugar
- 1 teaspoon ground cinnamon
- ½ teaspoon grated nutmeg
- 1 tablespoon honey
- Grated zest and juice of 1 lemon
- 3 eggs
- 3 tablespoons fine matzo meal (cake meal)
- 125 g/4 oz pareve margarine, melted
- 1 tablespoon sugar
- 2 tablespoons marmalade or apricot preserve

☐ Into a large bowl, place broken matzo pieces. Cover with cold water and leave to stand until slightly softened, 10 minutes. Drain well and mash with a fork until almost smooth.

☐ Preheat oven to 180°C/350°F/Gas Mark 4. Lightly grease a 20 to 23.5 cm/8 or 9 in square, deep baking dish. Add grated apple or pear, raisins, apricots and almonds or walnuts to matzo and mix well. Stir in half the sugar, cinnamon, nutmeg, honey and lemon zest and juice.

☐ In a medium bowl, beat eggs with remaining sugar until thick and creamy and sugar is dissolved, 3 to 5 minutes. Beat into matzo mixture until well blended. Stir in half the melted margarine and scrape into the baking dish, smoothing top evenly.

☐ Drizzle remaining margarine over top and sprinkle with 1 tablespoon sugar. Bake until a knife inserted in the centre comes out clean and top is browned and slightly puffed, 1 hour.

☐ In a small saucepan, over medium heat, heat marmalade or apricot preserve with 1 tablespoon water. When pudding is baked, brush mixture over the top and cool pudding at least 15 minutes before serving.

ABOVE A STREET VENDOR SELLING BAKED GOODS IN ISTANBUL, TURKEY.

Sliced Exotic Fruits with Dates

SERVES 6

Fruit salad has always been a popular dessert in Jewish homes because it is neutral; it is welcome after meat or milk meals. Almost any seasonal fruits are delicious sliced or cut up together in their natural juices or with a fruit purée. This is not a traditional fruit salad, but a selection of exotic fruits, sliced and served together. Ogen melons from Israel are as sweet as sugar, as are the Israeli oranges. Dates are popular throughout the Middle East, but California produces a wonderful variety, the Medjool date, which I recommend for this dish.

- 1 Ogen melon, seeded and sliced in thin wedges and peeled
- 3 sweet seedless oranges, peeled and segmented, juice reserved
- 1 mango, peeled and thinly sliced
- 24 fresh lychees, peeled, or 1 425 g/14 oz can lychees in their own juice
- 12 Medjool dates, cut in half lengthwise and stoned
- 1 pomegranate, cut in half, seeds reserved (optional)
- Fresh mint leaves for garnish

☐ Arrange slices of melon on each of 6 individual plates in a fan shape. Arrange peeled orange segments and mango slices in an attractive pattern over the melon slices.

☐ Evenly distribute fresh or canned lychees over fruit and sprinkle on some reserved juices from all fruits.

☐ Arrange 4 date halves on each plate and sprinkle over the pomegranate seeds, if using. Garnish with fresh mint leaves and serve.

Baked Goods

Lemon-Scented Plava

Easy Chocolate Passover Roulade

New York-Style Cheesecake

Lekach

"Jewish" Apple Cake

Sufganiyot

Coconut Macaroons

Hamantaschen

Easy Cinnamon Balls

Walnut-Raisin Rugelach

Moroccan Butter Biscuits

Mandelbrot

Pecan-Cinnamon Buns

Quick-and-Easy Babke

Butter Kuchen

Bagels

Sesame Pita Bread

Kubaneh

Old-Fashioned Rye Bread

Challah

LEMON-SCENTED PLAVA

SERVES 6 TO 8

Passover cakes are probably the most uniquely Jewish of all cakes, because they are made with flour substitutes. These cakes were perfected by the Sephardic Jews in Spain who escaped to Greece during the Inquisition, but they are now enjoyed by Jews the world over. The most popular substitutes are potato flour, very fine matzo meal sometimes called cake meal, and ground nuts. The end result is a light, delicate sponge cake, served here with a lemon sauce.

- 6 eggs, separated
- 250 g/8 oz sugar
- 125 g/4 oz fine matzo meal (cake meal)
- 60 g/2 oz finely ground blanched almonds or potato flour
- ¼ teaspoon ground cinnamon
- Grated zest and juice of 1 lemon
- Almond halves or slivered almonds for decoration

FOAMY LEMON SAUCE

- 1 tablespoon arrowroot
- 150 g/5 oz sugar
- Grated zest and juice of 1 lemon
- 2 eggs, separated

☐ Preheat oven to 180°C/350°F/Gas Mark 4. Grease a 21 to 23.5 cm/8½ to 9 in springform cake tin. In a large bowl, with an electric mixer, beat egg yolks with half the sugar until thick and lemon coloured and mixture forms a "ribbon" when beaters are lifted from bowl, 3 to 5 minutes.

☐ In another large bowl, with cleaned beaters, beat egg whites until soft peaks form. Gradually beat in remaining sugar, in 3 or 4 batches, beating well after each addition, until whites form stiff peaks.

☐ In a medium bowl, combine matzo meal, ground almonds or potato flour, cinnamon and lemon zest. Alternately, in 3 batches, fold beaten whites and matzo-almond mixture gently into the beaten yolks. Fold in lemon juice.

☐ Pour mixture into prepared tin and press almond halves into mixture at 5 cm/2 in intervals or sprinkle with slivered almonds.

☐ Bake until top is golden and skewer inserted in centre comes out clean, 45 to 55 minutes. Remove to wire rack to cool 10 minutes. Carefully run a sharp knife around edge of tin to loosen edges, then unclip side of tin and remove. Cool completely; cake may sink a little.

☐ Prepare Foamy Lemon Sauce. In a medium saucepan, combine arrowroot and sugar. Slowly stir in 375 ml/12 fl oz water and lemon zest and juice, until well blended and smooth. Beat in egg yolks.

☐ Over medium-low heat, cook mixture until slightly thickened, 3 to 4 minutes. Bring to a boil, then remove from heat.

☐ In a medium bowl, with electric mixer, beat whites until soft peaks form. Slowly fold in yolk mixture until just blended. Cool, then refrigerate at least 1 hour or until chilled. Serve cold with cake.

Easy Chocolate Passover Roulade

SERVES 10 TO 12

Sponge cakes are often served at Passover when leavening agents are not used. This easy cake is ideal for any time of the year. If you do not eat chestnuts, sweetened whipped cream or any favourite filling can be substituted.

- 175 g/6 oz good-quality plain chocolate, chopped
- 60 ml/2 fl oz strong coffee
- 6 eggs, separated
- 75 g/2½ oz sugar
- 2 teaspoons vanilla extract
- Cocoa powder
- Icing sugar
- *Marrons glacés* for garnish

CHESTNUT FILLING

- 450 ml/¾ pt double or whipping cream
- 2 tablespoons coffee-flavour liqueur, or 2 teaspoons vanilla or rum extract
- 450 ml/¾ pt canned sweetened chestnut purée

☐ Preheat oven to 180°C/350°F/Gas Mark 4. Grease a 38 × 26 cm/15½ × 10½ in Swiss-roll tin; line with greaseproof paper, then grease and flour paper. In a small saucepan, over low heat, melt chopped chocolate with coffee, stirring until smooth and well blended. Set aside and cool slightly.

☐ In a large bowl, with electric mixer, beat egg yolks with half the sugar until pale and thick, 4 to 5 minutes. Beat in cooled chocolate until just blended.

☐ In another bowl, with cleaned beaters, beat egg whites until soft peaks form. Gradually beat in remaining sugar, 1 teaspoon at a time, beating well after each addition until stiff peaks form. Beat in vanilla.

☐ Stir a large spoonful of whites into chocolate-yolk mixture to lighten it, then fold into remaining whites. Spoon into prepared tin, smoothing top evenly. Bake until cake springs back when lightly pressed with a finger, 12 to 15 minutes.

☐ Dust a clean tea towel with cocoa powder. When cake is baked, immediately turn out on to tea towel and remove paper. Starting at a narrow end, roll cake and towel together Swiss-roll fashion. Remove to wire rack to cool completely.

☐ Make filling. In a large bowl, beat cream and liqueur or extract until soft peaks form. Beat a large spoonful of cream into chestnut purée to lighten it, then fold in remaining cream. Unroll cake and spread chestnut mixture to within 2.5 cm/1 in of edges. Using towel to lift cake, reroll cake Swiss-roll fashion.

☐ Decorate roulade with bands of sifted icing sugar. Carefully slide cake on to a long serving plate. If you like, decorate with *marrons glacés*.

NEW YORK-STYLE CHEESECAKE

SERVES 8 TO 10

Baked cheese recipes can be traced back to the discovery of curd cheese in the Middle East centuries ago. Western cheesecake as we know it is probably a descendant of the Russian Easter pashka, a tall moulded dessert of homemade cottage cheese, eggs, sugar, sour cream, butter and chopped nuts. This dense, smooth, lemony cheesecake is heavenly and perfect for a Shavuot dessert.

- 20–22 digestive biscuits, crushed
- ½ teaspoon ground cinnamon
- 45g/1½ oz butter or margarine, melted
- 750 g/1½ lb cream cheese
- 175 g/6 oz sugar
- Grated zest of 1 lemon
- 1 teaspoon vanilla extract
- 3 eggs

SOUR CREAM TOPPING

- 250 ml/8 fl oz sour cream
- 2 tablespoons sugar
- 1 teaspoon vanilla extract

☐ Preheat oven to 180°C/350°F/Gas Mark 4. Lightly butter a 23.5 cm/9 in springform cake tin. In a medium bowl, combine biscuit crumbs, cinnamon and butter or margarine. Press crumbs on to bottom and 4 cm/1½ in up sides of tin. Bake 5 minutes until just set. Remove to a wire rack to cool.

☐ In a large bowl, with an electric mixer on medium-low speed, beat cream cheese with sugar until smooth. Add lemon zest and vanilla, then beat in eggs, 1 at a time, until batter is well blended and smooth.

☐ Carefully pour filling into cooled crust. Bake until firm at edges but still slightly soft in centre, 45 to 50 minutes. Do not allow cake to brown; it should be puffed and slightly golden. Turn off oven and leave cheesecake in oven with door closed for 1 hour. (This helps prevent the surface from cracking.) Remove to wire rack, cool.

☐ Preheat oven to 220°C/425°F/Gas Mark 7. Make topping. In a small bowl, combine sour cream, sugar and vanilla. Carefully pour over top of cake and return to oven. Bake 5 minutes. Remove cake to wire rack to cool completely. Refrigerate overnight.

☐ To serve, run a sharp knife around edge of tin to loosen edges. Carefully remove side of springform tin and place cake on serving dish.

ABOVE One of the many Jewish food emporia in New York City.

VARIATION

STRAWBERRY CHEESECAKE

Prepare cheesecake as above, but before serving, decorate edge of cake with strawberries hulled and cut in half lengthwise. In a food processor fitted with metal blade, process 300 g/10 oz frozen strawberries in light syrup, or 500 g/1 lb fresh strawberries, hulled, and 3 tablespoons sugar to taste. Sieve and add a little lemon juice or water to thin if necessary. Serve separately with cheesecake.

LEKACH

SERVES 12

This honey cake is the traditional Jewish New Year's cake. Sweet honey as we know it did not really become available until Roman times and even then was prized for its medicinal uses and saved for joyful holidays and special occasions. Lekach, Yiddish for honey cake, or *pain d'épices* (spice bread) as it is called in France, is heavily flavoured with ginger and other spices and resembles the German-style gingerbread, although that cake uses molasses instead of honey. This is my sister-in-law's recipe, the most popular in the family.

- 300 g/10 oz plain flour
- 125 g/4 oz wholemeal flour
- 125 g/4 oz dark brown sugar
- 1 tablespoon baking powder
- 1 teaspoon bicarbonate of soda
- 2 teaspoons ground ginger
- 1 teaspoon ground cinnamon
- ½ teaspoon ground allspice
- 60 g/2 oz walnuts or almonds, chopped and toasted (optional)
- 90 g/3 oz sultanas (optional)
- 425 ml/14 fl oz honey
- 250 ml/8 fl oz strong black coffee
- 3 tablespoons bourbon whisky, brandy or water
- 4 eggs
- 60 ml/2 fl oz vegetable oil
- 8 tablespoons ginger preserve or chopped stem ginger in syrup
- Icing sugar for dusting or honey for glazing

☐ Preheat oven to 180°C/350°F/Gas Mark 4. Grease a 23.5 × 32.5 cm/9 × 13 in cake tin; line with greaseproof paper; grease and flour paper.

☐ In a large bowl, combine flours, sugar, baking powder, bicarbonate of soda, ginger, cinnamon and allspice. Stir in chopped walnuts or almonds and sultanas if using. Set aside.

☐ In a small saucepan, over medium-low heat, heat honey with coffee until warm and remove from heat. Stir in bourbon whisky, brandy or water.

☐ In a large bowl, beat eggs with vegetable oil until well blended. Beat in ginger preserve or stem ginger. Alternately, in 3 or 4 batches, stir warm honey mixture and flour mixture into the beaten egg mixture until well blended.

☐ Pour mixture into prepared tin. Bake until skewer inserted in centre comes out with just a few crumbs attached and top springs back when gently pressed with a finger, 1 hour. Remove tin to wire rack and cool completely.

☐ Turn out cake on to a rack and then back on to serving plate, so cake is right side up. Dust with icing sugar or, if you do not mind a sticky cake, brush with slightly heated honey, and cut into squares to serve.

"JEWISH" APPLE CAKE

SERVES 16 TO 20

Apple cake made with oil is a popular choice for a Hanukkah cake because the oil symbolizes the holiday's miracle. These layers of tangy apples baked in a moist, sweet, lemon-scented mixture make this one of my favourite cakes. My sister-in-law uses this recipe, and I love it when she serves it at tea time.

APPLE FILLING

- 1 kg/2 lb cooking apples, peeled, cored and thinly sliced
- 4 tablespoons sugar
- 1 teaspoon ground cinnamon
- Grated zest and juice of 1 lemon

CAKE

- 4 eggs
- 250 g/8 oz caster sugar
- 250 ml/8 fl oz vegetable oil
- 250 g/8 oz self-raising flour, or use plain flour plus 2 teaspoons baking powder
- 1 teaspoon vanilla extract
- Sugar for sprinkling

☐ Preheat oven to 180°C/350°F/Gas Mark 4. Grease a 23.5 × 32.5 cm/9 × 13 in cake tin. In a large bowl, toss apple slices with sugar, cinnamon, lemon zest and juice.

☐ In a large bowl, with electric mixer at medium speed, beat eggs with sugar until thick and lemon coloured and mixture forms a "ribbon" when beaters are lifted from bowl, 3 to 5 minutes. Beat in oil until well blended. Stir in flour and vanilla just until well mixed and smooth.

☐ Pour half the mixture into prepared tin. Spoon half the apple slices over mixture. Cover apple slices with remaining mixture; top with remaining apple mixture. Sprinkle with about 2 tablespoons sugar.

☐ Bake until apples are tender and cake is golden brown and puffed and top springs back when gently pressed with a finger, 1¼ to 1½ hours. Cover with foil during baking if top colours too quickly. Remove to wire rack to cool. Cut cake into squares and serve at room temperature.

SUFGANIYOT

MAKES 24

These jam-filled doughnuts were eaten by many Ashkenazic Jews in Central and Eastern Europe, and are now very popular in Israel at Hanukkah because they are fried in oil. Fried sweet fritters have a long history among Sephardic Jews and are probably descended from the Greek loukomades, a fritter which was dipped in a honey syrup.

- 2 tablespoons dried yeast
- 2 tablespoons sugar
- 300 ml/½ pt lukewarm milk
- 4 egg yolks
- 500 g/1 lb strong plain flour
- ¼ teaspoon salt
- Vegetable oil for frying
- Plum, apricot, redcurrant or blackcurrant jam
- Caster sugar for coating

☐ In the bowl of an electric mixer fitted with dough hook, combine yeast, sugar and lukewarm milk. Stir 1 minute, then leave to stand until the surface begins to look bubbly and foamy, 10 to 12 minutes. With mixer on low speed, beat in egg yolks.

☐ Add flour and salt and mix until a soft dough forms. Knead until dough is smooth and elastic and clings to the dough hook, 4 to 6 minutes. Lightly grease a bowl and place dough in it, turn to coat dough with oil. (This prevents a crust from forming on surface of the dough.)

☐ Cover bowl with a clean tea towel and leave in a warm place until doubled in bulk, 1½ to 2 hours. Turn out dough on to floured surface and roll out about 2 cm/¾ in thick. Using a 5 cm/2 in floured cutter, cut out 24 or more circles. Dust with a little flour and cover with tea towel; leave until puffy and risen, 20 to 30 minutes. (Knead scraps together and return to bowl for 20 to 30 minutes to rise again; reroll and cut.)

☐ Fill a deep-fat fryer or large saucepan with 7.5 cm/3 in oil and, over medium-high heat, heat to 180°C/350°F to 185°C/360°F. Fry doughnuts in batches 3 to 4 minutes on each side. Do not crowd or temperature of oil will drop and doughnuts will absorb too much oil. With a slotted spoon, remove to paper towels to drain.

☐ Fill a small piping bag fitted with a 1.25 cm/½ in plain nozzle with jam. When cool enough to handle, make a small slit in side of each doughnut. Insert nozzle into a doughnut and squeeze about 1 teaspoon of the jam into centre.

☐ Into a small shallow dish, place 125 g/4 oz sugar. Roll each filled doughnut in the sugar to coat on all sides. Serve warm.

ABOVE MAGNIFICENTLY LIT INTERIOR OF AN OLD SYNAGOGUE IN MOSCOW.

Coconut Macaroons

MAKES ABOUT 30

These are an easy Passover biscuit, very popular in the United States as they store well and taste delicious. Of course, all macaroons are a good way to use extra egg whites.

- 4 egg whites
- ¼ teaspoon cream of tartar
- 250 g/8 oz sugar
- 1 teaspoon lemon juice or distilled white vinegar
- 1 teaspoon vanilla extract
- 275 g/9 oz desiccated coconut.

☐ In a large bowl, with electric mixer at medium speed, beat whites until frothy. Add cream of tartar and beat on high speed until firm peaks form. Gradually sprinkle in sugar, 2 tablespoons at a time, beating well after each addition until whites form stiff peaks.

☐ Sprinkle lemon juice or vinegar, vanilla and coconut over whites. Gently fold in until just blended.

☐ Preheat oven to 150°C/300°F/Gas Mark 2. Line 2 baking sheets with baking parchment. Drop mixture by heaped teaspoonful, keeping a cone shape, about 2.5 cm/1 in apart.

☐ Bake 40 to 45 minutes until lightly browned; macaroons should be *very* slightly soft in centre. Remove macaroons on paper to wire rack to cool slightly. Carefully peel off paper and cool completely. Store in an airtight container.

HAMANTASCHEN

MAKES ABOUT 30

Also called "haman's ears", these are little three-cornered biscuits which have become the traditional Ashkenazic Purim sweet. They can be made from a yeast-based dough or an easy biscuit-dough base. The most traditional fillings are poppy seeds or prunes.

BISCUIT DOUGH

- 150 g/5 oz unsalted butter or margarine, softened
- 125 g/4 oz sugar
- 1 egg
- 3 tablespoons milk or water
- ½ teaspoon vanilla extract
- 250 to 300 g/8 to 10 oz plain flour
- 1 teaspoon baking powder

POPPY SEED-HONEY FILLING

- 300 g/10 oz poppy seeds, whole or ground
- 125 ml/4 fl oz honey
- 60 g/2 oz light brown sugar
- ⅛ teaspoon salt
- 30 g/1 oz walnuts or blanched almonds, finely chopped (optional)
- 1 tablespoon lemon juice
- ½ teaspoon grated lemon zest
- 1 egg, beaten, for glaze (optional)

VARIATION

PRUNE-FILLED HAMANTASCHEN

SOMETIMES CALLED LACQUA, THIS IS REALLY A PRUNE BUTTER. COMBINE 300 TO 425 G/10 TO 14 OZ CHOPPED PITTED PRUNES, GRATED ZEST AND JUICE OF 1 ORANGE AND 250 ML/8 FL OZ WATER IN A SAUCEPAN. COOK OVER MEDIUM HEAT UNTIL SOFT, 5 MINUTES. REMOVE FROM HEAT AND COOL SLIGHTLY. MASH PRUNE MIXTURE BY HAND OR PURÉE IN A FOOD PROCESSOR FOR FINE PASTE. STIR IN 2 TABLESPOONS PLUM OR APRICOT JAM. PREPARE DOUGH AND FILL AND BAKE AS ABOVE.

☐ In a medium bowl, with electric mixer, cream butter or margarine and sugar until smooth and well blended. Add egg, milk or water and vanilla and beat until smooth and creamy.

☐ Combine flour and baking powder, then gently stir into butter mixture until well blended.

☐ Turn out dough on to lightly floured surface and knead lightly to blend. Form into a ball, flatten and wrap tightly. Refrigerate until completely firm, 3 to 4 hours or overnight.

☐ Make filling. In a medium saucepan, over medium-low heat, cook poppy seeds, 125 ml/4 fl oz water, honey, brown sugar and salt until thickened to a soft pastelike consistency, stirring frequently, 5 minutes. Remove from heat and cool slightly. Stir in chopped nuts, if using, and lemon juice and zest.

☐ Preheat oven to 190°C/375°F/Gas Mark 5. Lightly grease 2 baking sheets. Place dough on lightly floured surface and cut in half; refrigerate one half. Roll out dough 3 mm/⅛ in thick. Using a 5 cm/2 in round cutter, cut as many circles as possible. Lightly brush edge of dough with water and place 1 teaspoon poppy seed filling in centre of each. Pull up edges in three equidistant places to form a triangle. Pinch edges together, leaving a tiny space open along each side.

☐ Place dough triangles on baking sheet about 2.5 cm/1 in apart. Brush with the egg glaze, if you like. Bake until golden brown, 14 to 18 minutes. Remove to wire rack to cool. Repeat with remaining dough. Store biscuits in an airtight container.

ABOVE Scuba diving and windsurfing in the Red Sea, Israel.

Easy Cinnamon Balls

MAKES ABOUT 20

These biscuits were so easy my brothers and I were allowed to make them when we were quite young. We could not go close to the oven and the size of the biscuits was never uniform, but we all had a good time; part of the joy of Passover.

- 250 g/8 oz blanched almonds or walnuts, finely ground
- 250 g/8 oz sugar
- 1 tablespoon ground cinnamon
- 2 egg whites
- ⅛ teaspoon cream of tartar
- Icing sugar and cinnamon for rolling

☐ Preheat oven to 170°C/325°F/Gas Mark 3. Lightly grease a large baking sheet. In a medium bowl, combine ground almonds or walnuts, 125 g/4 oz sugar and cinnamon. Set aside.

☐ In another medium bowl, with electric mixer, beat whites until frothy. Add cream of tartar and continue beating until soft peaks form. Gradually add remaining sugar, 1 tablespoonful at a time, beating well after each addition, until whites are stiff and glossy. Gently fold in nut mixture.

☐ With wet hands, shape mixture into walnut-size balls. Place on baking sheet about 25 cm/1 in apart. Bake until golden brown and set, 25 to 30 minutes. Remove baking sheet to wire rack to cool slightly.

☐ In a small bowl, combine 125 g/4 oz icing sugar and ¼ teaspoon cinnamon until well blended. Roll each warm ball in mixture to coat, then set on wire rack to cool completely. Add more icing sugar and cinnamon if necessary. When cold, roll each ball again in sugar mixture.

COOK'S TIP

If mixture is too soft to roll, add a few more ground almonds or a little fine matzo meal to stiffen it.

WALNUT-RAISIN RUGELACH

MAKES ABOUT 60

Rugelach are one of the most popular Jewish pastries in the United States. Often made with a simple cream cheese pastry, these little filled crescents melt in the mouth. Crescent-shaped pastries became very popular in Vienna as the shape became the symbol of Austrian victory over the Turks, in the late 17th century, but rugelach may well have their origins in the Middle East and Sephardic communities. The fillings can vary from poppy seed to cinnamon and walnuts, to cheese or chocolate or commonly raspberry or apricot jam.

CREAM CHEESE PASTRY

- 250 g/8 oz unsalted butter, softened
- 250 g/8 oz cream cheese, softened
- 1 tablespoon sugar
- 2 to 3 tablespoons sour cream
- 250 g/8 oz plain flour
- ¼ teaspoon salt

FILLING

- 125 g/4 oz sultanas
- 125 g/4 oz walnuts, finely chopped
- 2 teaspoons ground cinnamon
- 75 g/2½ oz sugar

- Milk for glazing
- 2 tablespoons sugar mixed with ½ teaspoon cinnamon

☐ In a large bowl with electric mixer (or by hand), cream butter and cream cheese together until well blended. Add sugar and beat until smooth, then beat in sour cream and mix in flour and salt until a soft dough is formed. Shape into a ball and flatten to disc. Wrap dough well and refrigerate until dough is firm, at least 2 hours.

☐ Preheat oven to 180°C/350°F/Gas Mark 5. Lightly grease 2 large baking sheets. In a small bowl, toss sultanas and walnuts with the cinnamon and sugar to mix. Set aside.

☐ Place dough on lightly floured surface and cut into quarters; work with one-quarter at a time, keeping remaining dough refrigerated. Roll out one-quarter of the dough 3 mm/⅛ in thick. Using bottom of 25 cm/10 in flan tin, cut dough into a 25 cm/10 in circle. Sprinkle dough with about one-fifth of the filling to within 2.5 cm/1 in of the edge.

☐ With a long-bladed, sharp knife, cut dough circle into 10 to 12 equal wedges. Starting at the curved edge, roll up each wedge Swiss-roll fashion. Place each on baking sheet, point side down (to keep filling from escaping) about 2.5 cm/1 in apart, curving ends down to form a crescent shape.

☐ Brush each crescent with a little milk and sprinkle with a little sugar-cinnamon mixture.

☐ Bake until golden brown, 20–25 minutes. Remove pastries to a wire rack to cool. Repeat with remaining dough and reroll trimmings to make extra pastries. Store in an airtight container.

VARIATIONS

RASPBERRY-ALMOND RUGELACH

COMBINE 125 G/4 OZ GROUND ALMONDS WITH 250 G/8 OZ RASPBERRY JAM. SPREAD ONE-FIFTH OF MIXTURE ON DOUGH CIRCLE BEFORE CUTTING INTO WEDGES TO WITHIN 2.5 CM/1 IN OF EDGE. SHAPE AND BAKE AS ABOVE.

POPPY SEED RUGELACH

USE HAMANTASCHEN POPPY SEED FILLING (SEE PAGE 112), SPREADING ONE-FIFTH ON EACH DOUGH CIRCLE BEFORE CUTTING. SHAPE AND BAKE AS ABOVE.

MOROCCAN BUTTER BISCUITS

MAKES ABOUT 30

Butter biscuits flavoured with nuts are found in most national cuisines from Morocco to Mexico. The Greek kourabiedes, or shortbread snowball, are made with almonds; the Austrian kipferl is made with hazelnuts. These biscuits, eaten in Morocco on Purim, can be made with walnuts or almonds.

- 250 g/8 oz unsalted butter, softened
- 250 g/8 oz sugar
- 375 g/12 oz plain flour
- 45 g/1½ oz walnuts or almonds, finely ground
- Coarsely chopped walnuts to decorate (optional)

☐ In a large bowl, with an electric mixer, beat butter until white and creamy, 5 to 7 minutes. Add sugar and continue beating until very smooth and creamy, 4 to 5 minutes. Stir in flour and ground walnuts or almonds by hand until well blended and a soft dough is formed. If dough is too soft to handle, add a little more flour or chill until dough is firm enough to handle, 30 minutes.

☐ Preheat oven to 150°C/300°F/Gas Mark 2. Lightly flour large baking sheets, but do not grease. With lightly floured hands, divide dough into walnut-size pieces and roll into smooth balls. Place on baking sheets about 2.5 cm/1 in apart. Press a few walnuts on top of each ball.

☐ Bake until set, 20 to 30 minutes. Do not let biscuits overcook or brown at all; they should remain a creamy off-white colour. Remove to a wire rack to cool. Store in an airtight container.

MANDELBROT

MAKES ABOUT 36

Mandelbrot, meaning almond bread in Yiddish, are hard, almond biscuits, double baked to create a dry biscuit like the Italian *biscotti alla mandorla*. It is likely that this biscuit was introduced to the Italians by the Spanish Jews. These cookies are delicious with coffee or tea, or as in Italy with a sweet dessert wine – *vino santo*.

- 300 g/10 oz plain flour
- 2 teaspoons baking powder
- ¼ teaspoon salt
- 3 eggs
- 250 g/8 oz sugar
- 6 tablespoons vegetable oil
- Grated zest of 1 lemon
- 1 teaspoon lemon juice
- ½ teaspoon almond extract
- 125 g/4 oz blanched or slivered almonds, coarsely chopped

☐ Preheat oven to 180°C/350°F/Gas Mark 4. Grease 2 baking sheets. In a bowl, sift flour, baking powder and salt. Set aside.

☐ In a large bowl, with electric mixer, beat eggs with sugar until thick and creamy, 3 to 5 minutes. Beat in oil, lemon zest and juice and almond extract. With the mixer on low speed, slowly add flour mixture until blended. Stir in almonds and beat until the dough is smooth.

☐ Turn out dough on to lightly floured surface and knead lightly. Divide dough in half and form into 2 long, flat loaves about 7.5 cm/3 in wide and 2.75 cm/1¼ in high. Place 1 loaf on each baking sheet and bake until golden brown, 35 to 40 minutes.

☐ Remove loaves from oven and leave to cool 10 to 15 minutes. When cool enough to handle, carefully cut 1.25 cm/½ in diagonal slices, dough will be soft inside. Wipe baking sheets and return slices to baking sheet (you will need to bake in batches). Bake until golden brown on underside, 6 to 7 minutes, then turn slices; bake another 5 to 7 minutes until golden. Remove to wire rack to cool completely.

PECAN-CINNAMON BUNS

SERVES 16

These buns form a sweet, sticky, delicious coffeecake. They come from the German-Austrian tradition of yeast cakes but have become popular all over the U.S. as a coffee-break treat. This is my brother's favourite.

- 1 tablespoon dried yeast
- 2 tablespoons sugar
- 60 ml/2 fl oz lukewarm water
- 75 ml/2½ fl oz milk
- 30 g/1 oz butter or margarine
- ¼ teaspoon salt
- 1 egg, well beaten
- 2 teaspoons vanilla extract
- 250 g/8 oz plain flour

PECAN-CINNAMON MIXTURE

- 45 g/1½ oz butter or margarine, melted
- 4 tablespoons golden syrup
- 150 g/5 oz light brown sugar
- 1 teaspoon ground cinnamon
- 60 g/2 oz pecans, coarsely chopped
- 90 g/3 oz sultanas

☐ In the bowl of an electric mixer fitted with dough hook, combine yeast, 1 tablespoon sugar and lukewarm water. Stir until yeast begins to dissolve, 1 minute. Leave to stand until bubbles begin to form on the surface and mixture looks foamy, 7–10 minutes.

☐ In a small saucepan, over medium heat, heat milk, butter or margarine, remaining sugar and salt; bring just to a boil. Cool to lukewarm. Stir into the yeast mixture. With machine on low speed, beat in egg and vanilla. Slowly add flour until mixture forms a smooth dough. On medium speed, beat dough until smooth and elastic, 3 to 4 minutes.

☐ Lightly grease a bowl and place dough in bowl; turn dough to coat. (This prevents a crust from forming on the surface.) Cover with clean tea towel and leave in a warm place until dough doubles in bulk, 1 to 1½ hours.

☐ Grease a 23.5 cm/9 in square baking dish or tin with half the melted butter, for filling, and drizzle with half the golden syrup. In a small bowl, combine brown sugar and cinnamon, then sprinkle half over butter and golden syrup in bottom of dish. Sprinkle with half the pecans.

☐ Turn out dough on to lightly floured surface and knead lightly. Roll out dough into a 20 × 40 cm/8 × 16in rectangle. Spread dough with remaining butter, drizzle with remaining golden syrup and sprinkle with remaining sugar mixture, pecans and sultanas. Starting at one long side, roll up dough Swiss-roll fashion.

☐ With a sharp knife, slice "Swiss-roll" into 2.5 cm/1 in slices and place, cut side down, in dish. Cover with tea towel and leave in a warm place until doubled in bulk, 1 hour. Preheat oven to 170°C/325°F/Gas Mark 3.

☐ Bake 35 to 40 minutes until rolls pull away from side of tin. Remove to wire rack to cool 2 minutes, then turn out on to a shallow tin or serving dish. Using a fork, separate individual rolls from each other. Serve buns warm.

QUICK-AND-EASY BABKE

SERVES 8

Babke is an egg-rich yeast dough of Russian-Polish origins. A yeast cake of this type probably exists in every country; it certainly resembles the German kugelhupf, the Spanish bola and what Italian Jews call bollo. In any language, studded with raisins, nuts and candied peel, this makes a delicious tea or coffee bread. This is a very easy no-knead recipe, moistened with a rum syrup. (You may notice the resemblance to the French *Baba au Rhum*!)

- 125 ml/4 fl oz milk
- 60 g/2 oz sugar
- 1 tablespoon dried yeast
- 60 g/2 oz butter or margarine, softened
- 3 eggs
- 1 teaspoon vanilla or rum extract
- 315 g/10½ oz strong plain flour
- 30 g/1 oz almonds or walnuts, chopped
- 45 g/1½ oz raisins, soaked in hot water 10 minutes and drained
- 45 g/1½ oz candied orange or lemon peel

RUM SYRUP

- 125 g/4 oz sugar
- 2 teaspoons rum or vanilla extract

ABOVE Note the Star of David on the wall of this Jewish Yemini home, Samala, North Yemen.

☐ In a small saucepan, over medium heat, heat milk and sugar until bubbles form around edge of pan and sugar is dissolved, stirring frequently. Cool to lukewarm.

☐ In a large bowl of an electric mixer, combine yeast and half the milk-sugar mixture. Stir until yeast begins to dissolve, 1 minute. Stir in remaining milk and butter or margarine; it does not need to melt.

☐ With mixer at low speed, beat in eggs, vanilla or rum extract and flour; continue to beat until batter is soft and smooth. Cover bowl with clean tea towel and leave in a warm place until well risen, 1 to 1½ hours.

☐ Grease and flour a 23.5 cm/9 in to 25 cm/10 in ring mould. With a wooden spoon or palm of your hand, beat almonds or walnuts, raisins and candied orange or lemon peel into dough. Turn into prepared tin.

☐ Cover with tea towel and leave in a warm place until dough has risen almost to top of tin, 50 to 60 minutes. Preheat oven to 180°C/350°F/Gas Mark 4.

☐ Bake until top is golden brown and feels firm to the touch, 30 to 40 minutes.

☐ Meanwhile, make syrup. In a small saucepan, over high heat, combine sugar with 125 ml/4 fl oz water and bring to a boil, stirring to dissolve sugar. Remove from heat and stir in rum or vanilla extract.

☐ When cake is baked, remove to wire rack and with a fork immediately pierce top all over. Slowly pour syrup over the cake while still hot.

☐ Leave cake to stand until syrup is absorbed, 1 hour. Carefully remove cake to serving plate and serve warm or at room temperature.

BUTTER KUCHEN

SERVES 10 TO 12

Kuchen, Austrian-German-style coffeecakes, epitomize the type of cake preferred by the Central and Eastern European Jews. Taken to the United States by German immigrants, the best ones are still the ones found in old German-Jewish bakeries.

- 2 tablespoons dried yeast
- 175 g/6 oz sugar
- 60 ml/2 fl oz lukewarm milk
- 175 g/6 oz unsalted butter or margarine, softened
- 3 eggs, lightly beaten
- 250 ml/8 fl oz sour cream
- Grated zest of 1 lemon
- 1 teaspoon vanilla extract
- 675 g/1 lb 6 oz strong plain flour
- 1 teaspoon salt

FILLING

- 45 g/1½ oz butter or margarine, melted
- 1 tablespoon ground cinnamon
- 175 g/6 oz sugar
- 175 g/6 oz sultanas
- 90 g/3 oz candied lemon peel

GLAZE

- 3 to 4 tablespoons icing sugar
- 1 to 2 teaspoons lemon juice

☐ In a small bowl, combine yeast, 2 tablespoons sugar and lukewarm milk. Stir until yeast begins to dissolve, 1 minute. Leave to stand until bubbles form on the surface and mixture looks foamy, 7 to 10 minutes.

☐ In bowl of an electric mixer fitted with beaters, cream butter or margarine and remaining sugar until well blended and smooth, 2 to 3 minutes. Beat in eggs, sour cream, lemon zest, vanilla and yeast mixture.

☐ Scrape beaters and replace with dough hook. On low speed, slowly add flour and salt and beat until well blended and a soft dough forms. Increase speed to medium and knead dough until dough is smooth and elastic, 5 to 7 minutes.

☐ Lightly grease bowl. Place dough in bowl and turn to coat. (This prevents dough from forming a crust.) Cover bowl with a damp tea towel and leave in a warm place until doubled in bulk, 2 to 2½ hours. (Alternatively, cover bowl with tea towel and refrigerate overnight to allow dough to rise very slowly.)

☐ Lightly grease a large baking sheet. Turn out dough on to lightly floured surface and roll dough 1.25 cm/½ in thick into a rectangle at least 60 cm/24 in long; brush with melted butter for filling. In a small bowl, combine cinnamon and sugar, then sprinkle over dough. Sprinkle with sultanas and candied lemon peel.

☐ Starting at one long end, roll up dough Swiss-roll fashion and bring ends together. Pinch ends to form a ring and place on baking sheet. With a sharp knife or scissors, slash ring diagonally from outer edge halfway to centre edge at 7.5 cm/3 in intervals. (This allows dough to rise more evenly, shows filling and forms a decorative shape.) Cover with tea towel and leave in warm place until ring doubles in bulk, 1½ to 2 hours.

☐ Preheat oven to 190°C/375°F/Gas Mark 5. Bake until golden brown, 40 to 45 minutes. Remove kuchen to wire rack to cool.

☐ Into a small bowl, sift icing sugar. Stir in 2 tablespoons water and lemon juice to form a glaze. Thin with a little more water if necessary. Drizzle over warm kuchen and slide on to serving plate. Serve warm.

BAGELS

MAKES 1 DOZEN

Bagels are round rolls with a hole in the middle, symbolizing the continuous circle of life. It is difficult to trace the bagel's origin, but it is likely they are from Poland or Austria, as the word bagel could derive from the Austrian/German word *beugel,* meaning stirrup, or the German/Yiddish *beugel,* meaning a curved ring or bracelet. Whatever its origin, it is surely one of the most popular "Jewish" breads, eaten all over the United States for breakfast, brunch or snacks. It is most popular with cream cheese and lox, but nowadays it is home to just about any sandwich filling.

The original plain bagel (water bagel) is made from high-gluten flour and is lightly poached in water to reduce its starch content before being glazed and baked; this gives the bagel its distinct, chewy texture. The addition of eggs to the dough was an American idea, as are the variety of flavours, such as pumpernickel, cinnamon-raisin, poppy or sesame seed, onion, garlic or pizza! In the U.S. there are bagel bakeries in all big cities, some open 24 hours. In Canada, the dispute for the best bagel rages on between Montreal and Toronto.

In London, I think the best bagels still come from the East End. The old Jewish neighbourhood has just about disappeared, replaced by Bangladeshi immigrants, but one shop still remains, selling the old-fashioned, chewy-style bagel.

- 1 tablespoon dried yeast
- 2 tablespoons sugar
- 60 ml/2 fl oz vegetable oil or 60 g/2 oz margarine
- 1 teaspoon salt
- 500 g/1 lb strong plain flour
- 1 egg, lightly beaten (optional)
- 1 egg, well beaten, for glaze
- Poppy or sesame seeds (optional)

VARIATION

BAGEL CHIPS

SLICE DAY-OLD BAGELS LENGTHWISE, INTO THIN SLICES ABOUT 6 MM/¼ INCH THICK. BRUSH WITH MELTED BUTTER OR OIL AND SPRINKLE WITH SESAME OR POPPY SEEDS IF YOU LIKE. BAKE ON A GREASED BAKING SHEET IN A PREHEATED 190°C/375°F/ GAS MARK 5 OVEN UNTIL BROWNED AND CRISP, 4 TO 5 MINUTES. REMOVE TO WIRE RACK TO COOL. STORE IN AN AIRTIGHT CONTAINER.

☐ In a small bowl, combine yeast and 1 tablespoon sugar. In a small saucepan over medium heat, heat remaining sugar, vegetable oil or margarine and salt with 250 ml/8 fl oz water, stirring until blended. Pour into yeast-sugar mixture and stir until dissolved, 1 to 2 minutes. Leave to stand until surface becomes bubbly, 5 to 7 minutes.

☐ Into a food processor fitted with metal blade, place flour. With machine running, slowly pour liquid into flour until mixture forms a ball of dough. If using an egg, add egg with liquid. Continue to process 1 minute longer. Dough should be smooth and not sticky. Add a little more flour if dough is too soft and process 30 seconds longer.

☐ Lightly oil a bowl and place dough in bowl; turn to coat dough. (This prevents a crust from forming on the surface.) Cover bowl with a clean tea towel and leave in a warm place to rise until doubled in bulk, 1½ to 2 hours.

☐ Turn out dough on to lightly floured surface and knead 2 to 3 minutes. Divide dough into 12 equal-size pieces. Roll each piece into a log about 14 cm/5½ in long; wet one end slightly and shape into a ring, pressing ends together firmly. Arrange rings on a large, lightly floured baking sheet. Cover with tea towel and leave to rise until almost doubled in size, 20 to 30 minutes.

☐ Preheat oven to 200°C/400°F/Gas Mark 6. Bring a large saucepan filled with water over high heat, to a gentle boil. Carefully slide 3 or 4 bagels into the water and cook 1 minute. Remove to paper towel and drain; continue cooking bagels.

☐ Lightly grease 2 large baking sheets. Arrange 6 boiled bagels on each sheet and brush with a little egg glaze and sprinkle with poppy or sesame seeds, if using. Bake bagels until well browned and crisp, 20 minutes. Remove to wire rack to cool. Serve warm or cool completely, then reheat to serve if you like.

SESAME PITA BREAD

MAKES ABOUT 1 DOZEN

Pita, sometimes called pocket bread, is a Middle-Eastern flatbread. In the Middle East it is baked fresh everywhere; in the U.S. and Great Britain it is increasingly popular because of the large Greek and Indian communities. To get the effect of being baked in a clay oven, use a hot griddle or cast-iron frying pan. This is an ideal bread for weight-watchers as it does not contain any fat, but is full of flavour, especially this sesame version.

- 500 g/1 lb strong plain flour
- 1 teaspoon salt
- 1 tablespoon dried yeast
- 1 teaspoon sugar
- 375 ml/12 fl oz lukewarm water
- Sesame seeds for rolling

COOK'S TIP

TO HEAT SHOP-BOUGHT PITAS, PLACE ON A BAKING SHEET AND BAKE IN A PREHEATED 200°C/400°F/GAS MARK 6 OVEN 2 TO 3 MINUTES UNTIL HOT AND PUFFED.

☐ In a food processor fitted with metal blade, process the flour and salt 2 to 3 seconds to combine.

☐ In a measuring jug or medium bowl, combine yeast, sugar and 125 ml/4 fl oz lukewarm water, stirring, until yeast is almost dissolved, 1 to 2 minutes. Leave to stand until surface looks bubbly and foaming, 10 to 12 minutes.

☐ Stir 250 ml/8 fl oz lukewarm water into yeast mixture. With machine running, gradually pour in yeast liquid. If dough looks too dry, add a little water, 1 tablespoon at a time, and process until a ball of dough forms. Process 1 minute.

☐ Lightly oil a bowl, place dough in bowl and turn to coat with oil. (This prevents a crust from forming on the surface.) Cover dough with damp tea towel and leave to rise in a warm place until doubled in bulk, 1½ to 2 hours.

☐ Turn out dough on to lightly floured surface and knead lightly. Roll dough into a long, thick log and cut into about 12 equal-size pieces. Roll each piece into a smooth ball, flouring the surface only if necessary. Place balls on a floured baking sheet and cover with the tea towel. Leave to rise until doubled in bulk, about 30 minutes.

☐ In a small bowl, pour about 1.25 cm/½ in sesame seeds. Roll each ball into the sesame seeds to coat well; add more seeds to bowl as needed. On a lightly floured surface, roll each ball into a 12.5 to 15 cm/5 to 6 in circle.

☐ Preheat oven to 230°C/450°F/Gas Mark 8 or highest setting. Lightly flour 2 large baking sheets. Place 3 to 4 dough circles on each sheet and bake until just beginning to brown, about 3 minutes. Turn over and bake until lightly browned 2 to 3 minutes. Repeat with remaining dough. Serve.

ABOVE Blowing the *shofar* (ram's horn) on the Jewish New Year at the Western Wall in Jerusalem.

KUBANEH

SERVES 8

This Yemenite sweet bread is eaten on the Sabbath. It is a soft, semi-steamed bread which can be eaten with preserves or jams or as the Yemenites do, with a hot chutney-type relish or zhoug, a chilli-paste dip. Kubaneh can be baked in the oven or on top of the stove in a very heavy-bottomed saucepan.

- 1 tablespoon dried yeast
- 6 tablespoons sugar
- 500 ml/16 fl oz lukewarm water
- 500 g/1 lb strong plain flour
- 1 teaspoon salt
- ½ teaspoon ground cinnamon or ginger
- Margarine or butter, softened, for greasing

☐ In the bowl of an electric mixer fitted with dough hook, combine yeast, 1 teaspoon sugar and 125 ml/4 fl oz lukewarm water. Stir until yeast is almost dissolved, 1 to 2 minutes. Leave yeast mixture to stand until it looks bubbly and foamy on surface, 5 to 7 minutes.

☐ In a large bowl, combine flour, salt and cinnamon or ginger. With mixer on low speed, beat in 375 ml/12 fl oz lukewarm water until well blended.

☐ With machine on low speed, gradually add flour mixture and beat until mixture forms a soft dough. If mixture is very sticky, add a little more flour, but dough should be soft. Increase mixer speed to medium and knead until dough is very smooth but still soft, 5 to 7 minutes.

☐ Lightly oil a bowl. Place dough in bowl and turn to coat with oil. Cover with a clean tea towel and leave in a warm place to rise until doubled in bulk, 1½ to 2 hours.

☐ Turn out dough on to lightly floured surface and knead lightly to knock out air. Return to bowl, re-cover and leave to rise again in a warm place, about 1 hour longer.

☐ Preheat oven to 170°C/325°F/Gas Mark 3. Heavily coat a 25 cm/10 in ring mould with 45 to 60 g/1½ to 2 oz softened margarine or butter. Turn out dough on to lightly floured surface and knead lightly to knock air out. Divide dough into 8 pieces. Roll each piece into a ball. Place balls into bottom of mould just touching each other. Cover tin and leave in a warm place to rise again until balls form a ring, 30 minutes.

☐ Heavily grease a piece of foil large enough to cover tin; cover tin tightly. Bake until bread comes away from side of tin, 1¼ to 1½ hours. Carefully remove foil, lifting an edge facing away from you to allow steam to escape. If you like, continue baking, uncovered, to brown top, 15 to 20 minutes. Serve warm.

ABOVE FRESH GREEK BREAD BAKED WITH PRIDE.

OLD-FASHIONED RYE BREAD

2 LOAVES

Rye bread has become associated with Jewish-deli food to such an extent that the American bread producer Levy coined the slogan "You don't have to be Jewish to eat Levy's." Rye bread is, in fact, not specifically Jewish, but the Jewish Russian and Polish bakers who went to the United States during the great wave of immigration at the end of the 19th century, baked recipes from the old country and they inevitably became popular.

Rye flour is very low in gluten, so white flour is needed to lighten the texture and give the bread more body. It does make the dough more difficult to work with, so an electric mixer is helpful unless you are an expert bread maker.

- 5 cups all-purpose flour
- 3 cups rye flour
- 2 teaspoons salt
- 2 packages (2 tablespoons) active dry yeast
- 1 teaspoons sugar
- 2 tablespoons caraway seeds
- ⅓ cup vegetable oil
- 2½ cups lukewarm water
- 1 egg, beaten, or 2 tablespoons butter or margarine, melted, for glaze

VARIATION

PREPARE DOUGH AS ABOVE BUT FORM INTO 2 OBLONG, BULLET-SHAPED LOAVES, NOT ROUNDS. AFTER GLAZING, SLASH AND SPRINKLE WITH 1 TABLESPOON ADDITIONAL CARAWAY SEEDS.

☐ In a large bowl, combine flours and salt. Set aside. In bowl of an electric mixer fitted with the dough hook, combine yeast, sugar and caraway seeds. Add oil and 1 cup lukewarm water and stir, sprinkle with a little flour. Cover bowl with a clean dish towel and leave until mixture looks slightly foamy and bubbly, 10 to 12 minutes.

☐ With mixer on low speed, pour in 1½ cups lukewarm water and beat until combined. Gradually add flours; when completely incorporated dough will be sticky. You may have some flour mixture left over. Increase mixer to medium speed and knead dough until dough forms a soft ball around the dough hook and leaves side of bowl, 5 to 7 minutes. If dough remains very sticky, add a little more all-purpose flour and continue to knead 2 minutes. (Do not add too much more flour or bread will be tough.)

☐ Lightly grease a bowl and place dough in it; turn dough to coat with oil. (This prevents a crust from forming on surface.) Cover bowl with dish towel and leave to rise until doubled in bulk, 1½ to 2 hours, in a warm, draft-free place.

☐ Lightly grease a large cookie sheet. Turn out dough on to lightly floured work surface and knead gently to knock air out of dough. Knead lightly and cut dough in half and shape each half into a smooth round ball. Place each loaf on opposite corners of cookie sheet, flatten slightly and cover with a towel. Let loaves rise again until almost doubled in size, 1 hour.

☐ Preheat oven to 350°F. Brush loaves with egg glaze or melted butter or margarine. With a sharp knife, slash top of each loaf 2 or 3 times. Bake until loaves are well browned and sound hollow when tapped on bottom, 35 to 40 minutes. Remove to a wire rack to cool. (This prevents bottom from becoming soggy.)

ABOVE FRESH BAGUETTES IN A COUNTRY BAKERY IN NORMANDY, FRANCE.

CHALLAH

MAKES 2 LOAVES

Challah is the traditional, braided egg bread served on the Sabbath and other Jewish holidays. It is usually braided, except at Rosh Hashana when a special spiral loaf is prepared to symbolize reaching for heaven in the hope of a happy New Year. This is the most popular egg bread in the United States and one of the most versatile because its soft, yellow, cake-like crumb suits most foods very well.

- 1 tablespoon dried yeast
- 1 tablespoon sugar
- 75 ml/2½ fl oz lukewarm water
- 1 teaspoon salt
- 5 tablespoons vegetable oil
- 2 eggs, lightly beaten
- 750 g/1½ lb strong plain flour, sifted
- 1 egg, beaten with a pinch of salt and pinch of sugar, for glazing
- Sesame or poppy seeds

VARIATION

TO FORM THE TRADITIONAL ROSH HASHANA SPIRAL LOAF, PREPARE DOUGH AS ABOVE BUT ROLL EACH DOUGH HALF INTO 1 LONG SAUSAGE SHAPE ABOUT 60 CM/24 IN LONG AND 2.5 CM/1 IN IN DIAMETER. HOLD ONE END AGAINST THE SURFACE AND, USING IT AS THE CENTRE, BEGIN COILING THE SPIRAL AROUND ON ITSELF SO DOUGH FORMS CONCENTRIC CIRCLES. PLACE ON UPPER LEFT-HAND CORNER OF BAKING SHEET AND TUCK ONE END UNDER LOAF. REPEAT WITH SECOND PIECE OF DOUGH, PLACING IT DIAGONALLY OPPOSITE IT IN THE LOWER RIGHT-HAND CORNER OF BAKING SHEET AND BAKE AS FOR BRAIDED LOAVES.

☐ In the bowl of an electric mixer with dough hook fitted, combine yeast and sugar. Stir in water. Sprinkle with a little flour to cover. Cover with a clean tea towel and leave until mixture looks slightly foamy and bubbly, 10 to 12 minutes.

☐ With mixer on low speed, beat in salt, oil and eggs until well mixed. Gradually add flour; when completely incorporated dough will be slightly sticky. Increase mixer to medium speed and knead dough until dough forms a ball around the dough hook and leaves side of bowl, 5 to 7 minutes. If dough remains sticky, add a little more flour and continue to knead 2 minutes longer. (Do not add too much flour; a softer dough yields a moister loaf.)

☐ Lightly grease a large bowl. Place dough in it, turn dough to coat with oil. (This prevents a crust from forming on the surface.) Cover with a clean tea towel and leave to rise until doubled in bulk, 1½ to 2 hours, in a moderately warm, draught-free place; do not leave to rise in too warm a place or texture may be uneven.

☐ Turn out dough on to lightly floured work surface and knead gently. Return dough to bowl, cover tightly and refrigerate 6 to 8 hours or overnight to let dough rise slowly a second time. (Allowing dough to rise slowly provides a light, even texture.)

☐ Turn out dough on to a lightly floured work surface and knead gently. Shape into a ball and cut into 2 equal-size pieces.

☐ Lightly grease a large baking sheet. Working with one half at a time, cut dough half into 3 equal-size pieces; roll into balls. Roll each ball into long sausage shapes about 45 cm/18 in long and 2.5 cm/1 in wide. Braid the 3 sausage shapes together and place on one side of baking sheet, tucking ends neatly underneath loaf. Repeat with remaining dough to form second loaf.

☐ Cover loaves with clean tea towel and leave in a warm place to rise until almost doubled in size, 1 hour. Preheat oven to 190°C/375°F/Gas Mark 5.

☐ Brush each risen loaf with egg glaze and sprinkle with sesame or poppy seeds. Bake 40 minutes until loaves are well browned and sound hollow when tapped on the bottom. Remove to a wire rack to cool.

Apple cake, Jewish 109
Artichokes, Jewish Style 24
Avocado & Dill Sauce 66
Avocado & Pomegranate Salad 94

Baba Ganoush 22
Babke, Quick & Easy 118
Bean & Pasta Soup, Italian 32
Bagels 120
Bagel Chips 120
beef dishes
  Beef Tongue with Sweet-and-Sour Sauce 53
  Cholent 59
  in Kreplach 81
  Mexican Beef Tzimmes 54
  Old Fashioned Pot Roast with Onion Gravy 58
  Sweet-and-Sour Stuffed Cabbage 57
Beetroot Borsht 28
Beetroot Eingemacts 14
Beetroot-Horseradish Sauce 15
Beetroot & Watercress Salad with Mustard Vinaigrette 90
Blinis with Smoked Salmon & Sour Cream 38
Butter Kuchen 119

Cabbage, Red, Sweet-and-Sour 76
Cabbage, Sweet-and-Sour Stuffed 57
Cabbage Soup, Sweet-and-Sour 28
Calves' Foot Jelly 20
Carrot Salad, Mexican 92
Carrot Tzimmes Loaf, New Year 74
Ceviche 27
Challah 126
Cheese Blintzes with Strawberries 40
Cheesecake, New York-Style 106
Cheesecake, Strawberry 106
Chelou 86
Chestnut Cake Filling 105
chicken dishes
  Chicken with Walnuts & Pomegranates 46
  Classic Chicken Soup with Matzo Balls 31
  Cochin-Style Chilli Chicken 49
  Indian-Jewish Chicken 50
  North African-Style Poussins 48
  Spiced Roast Chicken with Matzo Stuffing 43
  Spicy Barbecued Chicken 45
chick-peas
  in Falafel 23
  in Hummus 24
Chocolate Passover Roulade, Easy 105
Cholent 59
Chopped Herring 18
Chopped Liver 19
Cinnamon Balls, Easy 113
Coconut Macaroons 111
Coffee Whipped Cream Cake Filling 105
Couscous, Quick & Easy 87
Couscous Stuffing 48
Cucumber Salad with Dill 93
Curried Fish fillets 65

Doughnuts (Sufganiyot) 110
Dried Fruit Compote 98
Duck, Israeli Roast 47

Egg dishes
  Haminados 35
  Egg & Onion 36
  Egg in Salt Water 14
  Scrambled Eggs with Lox 36

Falafel 23
Fidellos Tostados 83
Fingerheutchen (Thimble Noodles) 78
Fried Fish, Jewish Style 68
Fruit-Filled Lokshen Pudding 100

Gefilte Fish 64
German-Style Potato Salad 91
Goose, Roast, with Fruity Stuffing 44

Hamantaschen 112
Haminados 35
Haroset, Ashkenazic 13
Haroset, Sephardic 12
Herring, Chopped 18
Herring in Sour Cream 18
Horseradish & Beet Sauce 15
Hummus 24

Indian-Jewish Chicken 50
Indian Rice with Tomatoes & Spinach 84
Indian-Style Potatoes, Spicy 77
Israeli Roast Duck 47
Israeli Orange Sorbet 99
Israeli Salad 89
Italian Bean & Pasta Soup 32

Kasha Varnishkes 82
Kashrut 6, 8–9
Knaidle 59
Knishes, Cheese 26
Knishes, Potato 26
Kreplach 81
Kubaneh 123
Kugel, Savoury Noodle 79
Kugel, Sweet Potato & Parsnip 80

Lamb dishes
  Hamin 56
  Seniyeh 52
  Shashlik 60
  Stuffed Passover Lamb 62
Latkes 73
Lebnah 12
Leek Fritters 72
Lekach 108
Lemon-Scented Plava 104
Lentil Soup 30
Liver, Chopped 19
Lokshen, *see* Noodles
Lox (Smoked Salmon), Blinis with, & Sour Cream 38
Lox, Scrambled Eggs with 36

Mamaliga, Rumanian Style 84
Mandelbrot 116
Matzo Balls 31
Matzo Brei 37
Matzo Pancakes 37
Matzo Pudding, Favourite 101
Matzo Stuffing 43
Mexican Beef Tzimmes 54
Moroccan Butter Biscuits 115
Moroccan Carrot Salad 92
Mushroom & Barley Soup 30

Noodles (lokshen)
  Fidellos Tostados 83
  Fruit-Filled Lokshen Pudding 100
  Homemade Noodles 78
  Savoury Noodle Kugel 79
North African Poussins 48

Orange-Challah French Toast 38
Orange Sorbet, Israeli 99

Passover Lamb, Stuffed 62
pasta, *see* noodles
Pecan-Cinnamon Buns 117
Persian Pancakes with Yogurt 41
Peruvian Pickled Fish 27
Piroshki 17
Pita Bread, Sesame 122
Plaetschen (Noodle Squares) 78
Pomegranates, Avocado &, Salad 94
Pomegranates, Baked Trout with 69
Pomegranates, Chicken with Walnuts & 46
Pot Roast, Old Fashioned, with Onion Gravy 58
potato dishes
  German-Style Potato Salad 91
  Latkes 73
  Spicy Indian-Style Potatoes 77

Quinces, Oven-Baked 97

Red Snapper with Green Sauce 68
rice dishes
  Chelou 86
  Fidellos Tostados 83
  Indian Rice with Tomatoes & Spinach 84
Rugelach, Poppy Seed 114
Rugelach, Raspberry-Almond 114
Rugelach, Walnut-Raisin 114
Rye Bread, Old-Fashioned 125

Salmon, Baked, with Avocado & Dill Sauce 66
salmon, smoked, *see* lox
Savoury Noodle Kugel 79
Seniyeh 52
Shashlik 60
Shchav 32
Schmaltz & Grebenes 14
Shpaertzlen (Bow-Tie Noodles) 78
Sliced Exotic Fruits with Dates 102
sorrel 32
Strawberries, with Cheese Blintzes 40
Strawberry Cheesecake 106
Sufganiyot 110
Summer Fruit Compote 97
Sweet Potato & Parsnip Kugel 80
Sweet-&-Sour Cabbage Soup 28
Sweet-&-Sour Fish 70
Sweet-&-Sour Red Cabbage 76
Sweet-&-Sour Sauce, with Beef Tongue 53
Sweet-&-Sour Stuffed Cabbage 57

Tabbouleh 94
Tahini Sauce 15
Tongue, with Sweet-&-Sour Sauce 53
Trout, Baked, with Pomegranates 69
Turkey Schnitzel, Spicy 50
Tzimmes, Mexican Beef 54

Walnut-Raisin Rugelach 114
Watercress & Beet Salad 90

Zhoug 11

Zhoug 11